ADVAN(

"In this short book packed with wisdom and insightful advice, Dr. Klow delivers on his promise to help people realize that though they may be suffering in silence, they are neither 'crazy' nor unique, and that a therapeutic journey like the ones he offers his clients might be just the answer to their problems. As a seasoned therapist who secretly enjoys reading advice columns, I found this book a real page turner, as it offers sensible advice to people with problems ranging from unfinished business with parents, to breaking up with lovers, to finding meaning in life, and pretty much everything in between. Whether you are thinking of entering psychotherapy or just looking to see how an expert approaches some of life's thorny problems, this book will give you a taste of what that self-transformative journey might look like, and you may just recognize yourself in one or more of the book's excellent case vignettes."

Arthur Nielsen, MD, Professor of Psychiatry and Behavioral Sciences, Feinberg School of Medicine, Northwestern University, and faculty member at The Chicago Institute for Psychoanalysis and The Family Institute at Northwestern University

"Through compassion, deep psychological understanding, often enriched through metaphor, David Klow goes to the root of one's negative internal voices that often block better self understanding and enhanced relationships. He offers hope and healing opportunities through his integration of important psychological perspectives. This should be good reading for beginning and seasoned therapists, as well as clients."

Linda Rubinowitz, PhD, Licensed Clinical Psychologist, Licensed Marriage and Family Therapist, Assistant Clinical Professor, Department of Psychology, Senior Staff The Family Institute @Northwestern University

"In this superb book, David Klow shares letters he has written to his clients in psychotherapy. Klow's letters reveal the working of an outstanding therapist, and advance the use of writing to clients in therapy. These letters also capture the essence of good therapy, which above all else is about a caring shared interaction between clients and therapist. The wisdom communicated resonates broadly, well beyond the individual client to whom each letter is addressed. This is a magical volume sure to be of great interest to therapists, clients in therapy, and those who simply are engaged with the challenges of modern living."

Jay Lebow, Ph.D., ABPP, Senior Scholar and Clinical Professor, The Family Institute at Northwestern University

"*You Are Not Crazy* is a touching collection of honest and heartfelt letters written by David Klow to his clients. The book offers the readers a powerful look into the confronting issues many of us share, while also giving the readers a peek into the internal experience and processing of the therapist. David uses a compassionate voice while labeling what it is he sees in his clients. He challenges them, which often may feel like he's challenging you, to lean into vulnerability and bravely move through the healing. *You Are Not Crazy* leaves you feeling more connected to yourself and the world around you, while bringing forward a gentler inner voice for yourself."

Vienna Pharaon, LMFT, founder of Mindful Marriage and Family Therapy in New York, NY, and relationship expert for Motherly.

"Whereas most consumer oriented books on the subject of psychotherapy are guides that explain the techniques and principles undergirding the particular approach a therapist is taking, David Klow has offered clients an actual glimpse into the humanity of the therapist they sit with week after week. Klow is a deeply empathic companion to have on the journey toward self-understanding and healing. The book will encourage those who are contemplating taking the journey, as well as those already committed to the process."

Cheryl Rampage, PhD, Licensed Clinical Psychologist

YOU ARE NOT CRAZY

YOU ARE NOT CRAZY

Letters FROM YOUR *Therapist*

DAVID KLOW, LMFT

DISCLAIMER

This is a work of creative nonfiction. The letters are not to actual clients. Rather the individuals listed are an amalgam of various clients and people I have met over the years. They are composite characters. All names and identifying details have been changed to protect the privacy of individuals. Any events or clinical issues identified have been pulled from my work with various people over the course of many years. While the themes of my work are ubiquitous and common, any resemblance to actual individuals is purely coincidental.

Although I am a therapist, I am not actually your therapist. Reading this book does not create a therapist-client relationship between us. This book is not intended to be used as a substitute for actual psychotherapy with a trained clinician. The reader should consult with their doctor in any matters relating to their physical or mental health.

You Are Not Crazy
Letters from Your Therapist
David Klow, LMFT

ISBN: 978-1-942545-95-8
Library of Congress Control Number: 2017956611

www.wyattmackenzie.com
Contact us: info@wyattmackenzie.com

Dear Reader,

You are not crazy. Really, you're not. Others are experiencing nearly the same things as you. Yet they just don't talk about it. They often don't even have the words to describe what they are experiencing; but if they could, you might find that it is a lot like what you are going through. In other words, you are not alone. There is nothing wrong with you.

You see, the human condition these days is not only difficult, it is also isolating. So many of us think that we are the only one who is struggling. There is a sort of private shame that if others only knew the thoughts and feelings we are having, they would be shocked. Yet the secret is that they are having very similar thoughts and feelings themselves.

It is the human condition to have strange, dark ideations. It is normal to feel awkward, to yearn for all sorts of odd things and discordant experiences. We humans are a weird, lovely, and complex bunch. Most of us are evolving in ways that we don't quite understand. Yet from where I am sitting, this evolution is expansive and healthy and good.

Where I actually sit, day after day, is in a comfortable enough chair in a quiet enough room with individuals, couples, and families who are doing brave work to better understand themselves and their relationships with others. I am a therapist, and I watch as my clients struggle, grow, screw up, feel shame, and reach out for help. I join them as they succeed, overcome, and find unexpected inspiration. I go through a whole range of emotions each day. I cheer as my clients triumph. I cry with them as they fail and lose what they love. I lament their mistakes and celebrate their evolution.

There is so much I want to tell them each day, and I try my best to do so when I am in the room with them. Yet at times I can't always find the right words. I want them to know how much I care about their lives, how much I secretly root for them. I want to tell them how inspired I am by our conversations each week. The material that comes up in our work stays with me long after our sessions end. I learn from it, and my life is impacted by it.

I can't always find the right words in person. So I decided to write my clients letters after our sessions. It was my way of making sense of the work, of reaching out more deeply than I could to them in session. As I wrote the letters, they started containing insights and understandings that emerged from sessions, along with what I had been thinking and feeling during the time. My words were not always nice. Often I was compelled to confront a topic head on. My hope was that I had developed enough trust with the client, and that they knew I had tremendous compassion for them, before I was confrontational. If their therapist can't be honest with them, then who can?

This book is a collection of some of my letters. My hope in sharing them is that they might speak deeply to others with whom I don't have the privilege to meet in person. The names of the people in the letters, as well as aspects of their stories, have been changed to protect their privacy. While I've written these letters with a particular client, or clients, in mind, the topics are a composite of what shows up in all of their lives. This is a collection of themes, sentiments, and insights meant to soothe, inspire, and open new perspectives.

I sign these letters "fondly yours" because I am indeed fond of my clients, and I am truly theirs … at their service.

Most people long to have authentic, deep, and intimate conversations on a regular basis. They crave real, genuine conversations so that they can go deeper into themselves and connect more with the world. We are social creatures, and we need companionship in the process of our unfolding lives. With warmth, care, and deep wisdom, a heartfelt conversation (either in person, or in this case through letters) can inspire new possibilities in our lives.

I invite you, dear reader, to find yourself in these letters. Though I am writing to my clients, my wish is that somewhere in here, I am also writing directly to you. I offer these letters to you as a guide so that you might find inner resources you never thought you had. This book is not perfect, nor does it need to be. In fact, in our lives if we get stuck in pictures of perfection then we don't usually get much accomplished. Instead this book is an imperfect attempt to let you know that you are not alone, there is nothing wrong with you … and that you definitely are not crazy.

Fondly yours,
David

FOREWORD

DESPITE A SIGNIFICANT body of scientific evidence demonstrating its effectiveness, therapy remains shrouded in stigma. David has written a book which lifts the cloud of mystery and misunderstanding about asking for help. In *You Are Not Crazy*, David opens the door and invites his reader into the sacred space that is the therapy office. I suspect some readers will reach a tipping point as they travel through these pages and decide to begin therapy, having been offered a gentle preview of what is in store.

But David's book goes a step further. Readers journey not just into the therapy office, but into the therapist's internal world. By reading letters that David has written to his clients, readers have the rare opportunity to see the world through the eyes of a clinician. The perspective offered here is *heady*, as readers learn how negative life events knock us off course and how healing happens. The perspective offered here is also *heartfelt*, as readers are let in on something we don't talk nearly enough about—how much therapists really and truly care about their clients. *You Are Not Crazy* holds onto an important "both/and," which is that the practice of therapy is *both* how we earn a living *and* an authentic relational investment—an act of love. Inviting readers into that awareness will enhance the effectiveness of any therapy they undertake by inviting them to more deeply trust the very real intimacy of the relationship between therapist and client.

In the early pages of the book, David says, "We are social creatures, and we need companionship in the process of our unfolding lives." Seekers of therapy have, by and large, been wounded within the context of a relationship or relationships. This is the central paradox of life, isn't it? We need the closeness of people to grant our lives meaning, yet it is within the context of relationship that our greatest wounding occurs. Every page of this book honors that paradox. Our wounds tend to be relational wounds, and therefore, our healing must be relational as well.

Over 2,000 years ago, the Roman playwright Terence wrote: "*Homo sum, humani nihil a me alienum puto*", or "I am human, and I think nothing of which is human is alien to me." I am confident, therefore, that each letter will stir something in you. Some of these letters will stir a reaction that is akin to a ponder: "*Hmm, that's interesting*." Other letters will stir a reaction that is more akin to a powerful jolt: "*How did David get inside of my head?!*" The latter are the letters that you are advised to pay special attention to, as these letters shine a light on the places where your healing work lives. In my own book, I discuss how the first step toward making any kind of change is *naming* what the problem is. The letters in *You Are Not Crazy* are tools that will help you discover what in your life needs to be named. So often, our "dark and twisty" places (to quote Meredith Grey from *Gray's Anatomy*) stay wrapped in a heavy blanket of shame, but the letters in David's book remind us that we are not alone. No pain is new pain!

Readers will likely experience another kind of reaction as they read, which is the sense that a particular letter was written for someone in their lives—a spouse, partner, parent, sibling, coworker, or friend. When someone we care about is stuck in an unhealthy pattern, it takes a toll on us and we can begin to feel resentful and impatient. Observing the gentle way David reaches out to that type of person with that type of problem models a path of equanimity. The compassionate voice that David uses throughout the book will invite readers to consider moving past judgement to a place of empathy for the people in their lives who don't quite have themselves figured out yet.

I also love that this book will be read by therapists in training. Therapy is an art and a science, a craft which is developed over a lifetime. David's warm and wise voice is one that will offer tremendous benefit to clinicians who are early in their journeys, trying on frames and voices to see what fits. But seasoned therapists will find messages here for them, too! I have been practicing for over twenty years, yet I found on the pages of this book tools and frames that I will integrate into my clinical work.

You are not crazy. And you are not alone. Open yourself to the lessons offered in this book—lessons about pain and possibility, trauma and recovery, anger and forgiveness. You will be so glad you did.

Alexandra H. Solomon, PhD
Clinical Assistant Professor, Department of Psychology, Northwestern University
Licensed Clinical Psychologist, The Family Institute at Northwestern University
Author, *Loving Bravely: 20 Lessons of Self-Discovery to Help You Get the Love You Want*

TABLE OF CONTENTS

PART I
Starting Out on the Path

WHAT MAKES SOMEONE come in for therapy? Usually they are in some sort of pain that they don't quite know how to manage on their own. They are going through a divorce or breakup. Changes are happening in their home or professional life, or they are experiencing a significant amount of depression or anxiety such that they could use some support.

Pain is usually the greatest motivator that compels someone to seek therapy. Life's circumstances become overwhelming to the point where we could use some guidance, support, new insights, or even just someone who is in our corner as a trusted companion in the process. There is no shame in needing a little help. In fact, I think it is a sign of strength to be able to reach out for support.

What most people don't realize, however, is that the alleviation of psychological pain is just the beginning of the therapy process. There is so much more waiting for people to realize about themselves. While therapy certainly helps with the problems people come in with, what ensues is the beginning of a journey of self-discovery. Perhaps someone will come in dealing with a pending divorce, and we will work to help alleviate the pain from the loss. Then we start asking questions such as, "How did your relationship get here in the first place?" We will start down a path of inquiry, which usually leads to greater self-awareness.

This path of self-discovery and growth is an exciting one for me. I love the potential of what might happen when someone finally takes on their own personal development. Yet starting out on this path is not always easy. People need various tools in order to fare well in their quest for greater self-knowledge. They need some basic building blocks, such as increased self-care, or a more compassionate approach to their own mind. My goal is to help infuse our work with these tools, and then bring a new perspective to how people might approach their lives.

These first four letters are to those just starting out. They offer a basic orientation to therapy, personal growth, and self-care. When someone starts out on the path of self-discovery, they take significant steps toward wholeness. They take a stand for their well-being. It is the beginning of an important journey, one with twists and turns, yet which always leads toward health.

Dear Jenny: *What to Expect from Therapy*

Dear Jenny,

I think it is brave that you are coming into therapy. Your willingness to take on your own personal work, and start looking inside yourself, is commendable. A lot of people have misconceptions about what therapy is. They think it is what they have seen on television or movies. They assume that the therapist either has the answers, or worse, that the therapist sits there in judgment of their patients.

Neither of those portrayals is true. Instead, today's therapists take a more dynamic and collaborative approach to the work. We enter into relationships with our patients that we consider sacred. In the past, people thought therapy would "fix" them. They thought if they went to the therapist, they would be repaired, much like taking their car to the auto mechanic. Yet today, there is a new model of therapy emerging for the twenty-first century, and I thought it would be useful to share it with you so that it is explicit in our work.

Therapy can now be seen as a journey of self-discovery. A journey where you may realize strengths you thought you never had, and address weaknesses you thought you could not face. It is a place to be with what hurts within, while stepping into your full potential. In the presence of a nonjudgmental, compassionate therapist, you will have the opportunity to face these aspects of yourself so that you can find new ways of being.

There is really one reason to go to therapy. Whether the issue is anger management, anxiety, disconnection from life, children acting out, marital difficulties, addictive behaviors, or any number of concerns, the reason to seek therapy is clear. Therapy is an opportunity for transformation. Finding alternatives, growing into a new you, and changing old patterns of behavior can be a wonderful adventure. The question is, are you willing to take this journey of self-discovery and face the beautiful, as well as the not-so-beautiful, within?

Your relationship with your therapist is key. If you are willing to take this deep journey, you need a skillful, professional guide who can help. With such a guide, you can connect to a better understanding of yourself so that harmful patterns become retooled, reworked, and restored. An ideal therapist helps you see what needs to be developed and transformed within yourself. They can use a variety of methods to assist clients, including talk therapy, couples counseling, family therapy, archetypal imagery, energy work, meditation, and group therapy.

Research shows that regardless of the method, what makes counseling work is the relationship between therapist and client.[1] Developing a rapport can take a bit of time, but openness to developing this bond can really help. Nevertheless, people sometimes express that after a while nothing seems to be happening during therapy. After examining all possible barriers to the therapy working, you may have to be willing to go into parts of yourself that have previously not been explored. At this point, a shift usually happens: blaming others stops and you go further into your unknown strengths and weaknesses. New behaviors then emerge, which can help you function better in the world.

When therapy does not work, the question lingers, is it you or is it the therapist? Hopefully, as the therapist, I will be fully engaged in my own growth and development. Yet it is also up to you, the client, to take ownership of your therapy. The question is, how much responsibility are you willing to take for your own personal growth and change, and for that of your family? When therapy is effective, you and I are working together to create that change. When it's not, then it can feel stuck, flat, and disconnected.

In our work together, Jenny, my hope is that we will find a safe space to find answers. I hope that we can find ways for you to let go of old ways that are no longer serving you, and open new possibilities for you to step into the fullness of who you can be. It's not always the easiest process, but I'm up for it. It's a journey of sorts, and I really do look forward to this process with you.

Fondly yours,
David

Dear Susan: You Are Not Alone

Dear Susan,

I want you to know that you are not alone. While it feels like nobody really understands you, and that somehow you have been forgotten, I am here to tell you that this is not true. I can feel how your heart aches, and how lonely you are. I know how much time you spend by yourself, and how much you long for real companionship. I have seen how you experience so many life changes while barely sharing them with anyone. Yet even with all of this, I still want you to know that you are not truly alone.

You are part of something much bigger than yourself. While you live your life in what might feel like a solitary fashion, you are actually connected to many other like-minded beings who are going through very similar experiences. They may not interact with you in person, or speak to you directly, but they feel the things that you do. They too are moved to tears by moments of beauty. They ache and long in the same way you do, asking the same life questions into the ether. You are part of a team of open-hearted, sensitive, loving people who, through their own existence, make a big difference in this world. I talk with many of them each day. They tell me stories just like yours.

The big difficulty that I hear from so many of them is that they experience a separation from others. They feel disconnected from the world. Person after intelligent person has come into my office complaining of feeling alone. After a while I came to realize that it isn't just these particular people who complained of isolation. This is the human condition overall. Regardless of how many others are around us, the nature of the human mind these days creates an experience of separation and disconnection rather than a connected oneness with the flow of life. Though it may sound corny, Susan, you are not alone in feeling alone.

"Where are these other people?" you may ask. Why are they not in your life on a daily basis? Why don't they alleviate your loneliness, hold your hand, go for walks, or talk for hours with you? Susan, I am not sure. I really don't know why there is not satisfying, direct companionship in your life right now. I know that there have been way too many painful nights spent by yourself. Yet your ability to be on your own shows a great capability to love. It is contradictory that way, but being alone often allows us to connect more deeply. Osho says it quite nicely:

> *The capacity to be alone is the capacity to love. It may look paradoxical to you, but it's not. It is an existential truth: only those people who are capable of being alone are capable of love, of sharing, of going into the deepest core of another person—without possessing the other, without becoming dependent on the other, without reducing the other to a thing, and without becoming addicted to the other. They allow the other absolute freedom, because they know that if the other leaves, they will be as happy as they are now. Their happiness cannot be taken by the other, because it is not given by the other.*[2]

Your expectation that it will take loving intimate companionship to make you feel less alone is what gets you stuck. You fall into a sense of feeling that you are incomplete and separate from the world unless you have an adoring partner. Rather than looking for others to give you value or worth, I gently suggest instead that when you feel alone, you remember that you are already connected. You are not separate from the world. While not a substitute for the bliss of romantic love, if you find the quiet moments—the sensations of life: the flowers, trees, and plants; the animals, birds, music, and sound; the pulse of humanity around you—then you might come to feel that there's really no separation. You are a part of the world, right now, in this moment.

Life is waiting for you to connect more deeply. The door to this connection is inside you. There is no need to search far and wide for the relief to your loneliness. The answer is to go inside yourself and feel more deeply the life around you, to listen more carefully to the quiet whispers of connection. The world screams loudly around us, but life speaks softly for those who can hear. The ones who listen cannot help but express back into the world what they have heard, amplifying the love that runs like quiet groundwater through each of our lives. They are the artists, musicians, scholars, and teachers. They aim to reach each of us so that we might end our loneliness and fall once again into life's sweet embrace.

Whereas many search to feel more alive by partying, shopping, gambling, gaming, numbing out, or selling out, I invite you to instead turn inward to receive the thousands of blessings being showered upon you each day. Take in the songs, writings, and teachings of those who have gone before us. Find solace in their search for meaning and understanding. Find love and intimacy with humanity as a whole. Strive not to possess a companion to end your sense of separation, but instead seek to offer your love to those in this world who live alongside you.

Susan, you have so much to offer. I urge you to give your gifts, especially that of your kind and thoughtful presence. You, yourself, are the gift to give to the world. In offering who you are, you take steps to alleviate your loneliness. You come more from a perspective of abundant generosity, rather than the sense of deprivation that pervades so many of us who feel disconnected and alone.

Susan, when you forget that you are an important part of life, I will be here to remind you. Though we only meet for an hour once a week, I do carry you with me. I am in this with you. We are in this together.

Fondly yours,
David

Dear Martin: Take These Building Blocks

Dear Martin,

I have really enjoyed our first few meetings. You bring a particular openness and curiosity to the work in session. Instead of waiting until things are too overwhelming or painful, you have found your way to therapy, seeking better insight into who you are and why you do the things you do. I have enjoyed your proactive approach to counseling, and want to share with you some basic building blocks that may help make this process a bit easier.

First I want to share an old Buddhist story. It is about four horses. The first horse is very stubborn. It needs to be whipped repeatedly by its rider to move along at all. The second horse is resistant, too. This horse needs to be hit very hard, but only once, and then it starts running. Our third horse just needs the lightest tap from the rider to take off. Somehow this horse knows, or has learned, to respond to the gentlest of encouragement. Lastly, the fourth horse just needs to be shown the whip, and off it goes. Which horse are you?

The question here is not how obedient you are; rather, how much does life need to beat you down before you start to change? Do you need life's lessons to continually whip you until you move? Or can you get a sense from one or two painful experiences and change your ways? Most people hear this story and want to be the fourth horse. They want to avoid getting whipped repeatedly by life. Yet I would say that it doesn't matter which horse you are. We are all going to get moving along at some point. Life will find a way to make us grow. It is a matter of how much pain we need to endure before we learn how to make changes.

Pain is really the biggest motivator for people to seek therapy. Once they are in sufficient pain, they are humbled enough to ask for help. They approach therapy as something that will eliminate their pain. It certainly can, and often does, but therapy also offers so much more than just pain relief. It gives us a chance to better know who we are.

Socrates said, "Know thyself!" Prior to him, this saying was carved into the Temple of Apollo at Delphi. Knowing oneself has historically been seen as an all-encompassing knowledge, the cornerstone to living a meaningful life. Rather than coming to therapy to get over a breakup, or manage anxiety or depression, your interest in counseling, Martin, could be to better know yourself. I think this is a really great thing, but I have seen many well-meaning seekers stumble on the path of personal growth because they didn't have some of the basics down. They weren't practicing foundational skills that would allow them to grow, and their seeking just led to more pain. I want to share with you some of these building blocks for personal growth.

The first is to develop a kind inner voice. I tell this to all of my clients. Most of us are too hard on ourselves. Our inner voice is much more critical than it is supportive. Taking on the quest to know oneself is difficult enough, but being your own worst enemy makes it daunting. Many of us are quick to blame ourselves, or think painfully disparaging thoughts about our worth. While it is useful to pay attention to these negative thoughts and not empower them, it is equally useful to develop and build a more caring internal dialogue. In fact, it's essential for any sort of self-inquiry.

If you are going to make progress in therapy, then your self-care needs to include a compassionate, loving, and kind approach to your inner being. You need to treat yourself with a certain preciousness that honors your journey. Your inner voice needs to be encouraging, forgiving, and supportive. It needs to make room for changes and inconsistencies in who you are. Instead of beating yourself up, be tender and friendly to your own mind.

This affectionate inner dialogue is just an outcropping of an overall more compassionate approach toward yourself. Without compassion, you can't investigate who you truly are. This is the second building block. Having compassion for yourself is essential for personal growth and development. Without it, we end up being judgmental toward what we don't understand. We criticize ourselves for being strange or awkward. We reject who we are when we don't make sense. Instead of harsh scrutiny, our hearts need tender compassion. Being compassionate means gently accepting who we are, in a friendly way, with a curiosity toward understanding.

Knowing the difference between acceptance and permission is the third building block. Acceptance is different from permission. If we accept an unsavory aspect about ourselves, it doesn't mean that we then give ourselves free rein to act out. For instance, when you talked recently about being jealous of your partner's relationship with a coworker, you carried a lot of shame. You were ashamed that you felt jealous and acted in ways that were spiteful. The shame around checking the call log of your partner's phone, constantly questioning her, and looking into her coworker's background kept you from even understanding why you were even jealous in the first place. Rather than beat yourself up for this, if you can find room to accept your jealousy, then you might have a chance to change it. We could make a compassionate inquiry into why you are so jealous. Yet accepting that you are feeling jealous does not mean that you are giving yourself permission to keep behaving spitefully.

Instead your willingness to investigate what you feel is the next key building block toward knowing yourself. Your jealousy is not a reflection of you being a bad person. Instead, once we made some room for it, we found that it is an indication of a relationship that needs some healing. You and your partner have been distant lately. You haven't communicated well, and you have been afraid of losing her and being alone. We can have compassion for being afraid. It is understandable to be scared of loss. It is hard to let go; yet being able to do so, instead of acting out in a jealous way, can help.

Your ability to let go, when appropriate, is the last building block. When you are able to let go of who you have been, then you step into becoming who you might be. Can you release the person who is afraid of being alone? If so, then you create room for being someone who doesn't need to be jealous. This person isn't as afraid of losing the one he loves because he trusts. To be this person, you need to be open to previously unknown possibilities. Perhaps you never knew it was possible to trust in this way, regardless of the outcome.

Without dissociating from your thoughts and emotions, can you maintain a sense of detachment? Can you observe your inner life neutrally without overreacting to what you see? If you have a fleeting suspicion of your partner, you might start worrying. Then you become anxious about worrying, further fueling your fear. Instead, can you gently let go of the scared thought and watch your fear pass by? When we hold tight to our thoughts and emotions, they start to rule us. We may get swept away in a feeling of suspicion or jealousy. This inner letting go is invaluable as you start to know yourself.

I look forward to getting to know you more as well. It is incredibly wise and brave of you to start to take yourself on. Being prepared with these building blocks will help, and if you ever get stuck, I will to be there to help you find new tools to keep you going.

Fondly yours,
David

Dear Andrea: Real Self-Care

Dear Andrea,

I remember when we did a mini-role play in session. I played you, and you played your critical inner voice. While your portrayal of your critical inner voice could have won an Academy Award, it was rough to hear how you talk to yourself. Pretending to be you, it was unbearable for me to listen to how your critical inner voice berated you. Everything I tried to say in response was ripped to shreds by this brutal dictator inside of you.

Maybe dictator is too strong a word. Actually the voice felt like a very tough coach. The coach is trying to get the most out of you, but is going about it in such a punishing way. She urges you on, but also breaks you down. She does not trust that if left to your own devices, you would get things done. It is confusing, because the coach wants you to win, but is not very nice about achieving that goal. She doesn't care if you are reduced to a puddle on the ground, as long as the game is won.

We did some groundwork unpacking where this voice comes from. I think you understand that this voice was originally there to protect you, but got wildly out of control. Her job was to protect you from being too deeply impacted by other's criticism. Instead of being blindsided by someone else cutting you down, you were sure to get there first. You developed this voice in your preteen years, and unwittingly created a monster.

If someone, for instance, said, "Boy, you really aren't any good at the clarinet," you were ready to reply, "Yeah, I know. I stink."

You had already beaten others to the punch by sufficiently putting yourself down so that their criticism didn't sting as much.

"Nobody likes you," says some bully.

"Tell me about it," you reply. "I don't even like me!"

You get the point. This critical inner voice was initially there to shield your optimism from being squashed by the hard, cruel, naysaying world. We can't get rid of this critical inner voice, nor do we necessarily want to. It is there to protect you just in case. We just want to turn it down, and instead dial up your more supportive inner voice.

We have talked a lot about self-care. What do you need to do to take better care of yourself? Most people would say exercise, eat well, maybe even pamper yourself with a massage. Recently you said you were going to get your nails done and go to a specialty foods store that you have been meaning to visit. I thought those were perfectly good things to do to take care of yourself. However, if you were at the specialty foods store, looking at the many kinds of pretzels while your critical inner voice was telling you that you can't eat pretzels because of the gluten, and that you are getting too fat, and that your partner hasn't really seemed interested in you in a while, then it would really defeat the purpose of seeking self-care at the specialty foods store!

What is important is that your inner voice be caring and kind. Real self-care is having your interior monologue be loving and supportive. Yes, it is good to exercise, eat well, and pamper yourself, yet you must be caring in the way that you talk to yourself, too.

This is not about positive affirmations or mantras. This is about being deeply loving and kind in your thinking. It is about developing a healthy relationship with your own mind. Real self-care is embodying a compassionate response to whatever emerges from within you. It is kindly being with whatever thoughts and feelings exist within you. Usually those thoughts and feelings aren't too problematic in and of themselves. It is our response to the thoughts and feelings that cause trouble.

For instance, you might be driving and think, "Huh, I could just swerve this car right into the guardrail, and it'll all be over."

That's a pretty bad thought, but I have had it, and I know others have, too. Yet often we respond to that thought with, "Oh my goodness! I just had a horrible thought! What's wrong with me? Am I suicidal? That's horrible of me to have that thought. Bad! Bad! Stop thinking that!"

You see, the reaction to the thought about swerving into the guardrail was much more problematic and toxic than the initial thought itself. The first thought was random and scary, yet the second thought was tremendously punishing and critical. Most of us live with ourselves in the brutal fashion of the second thought year after year, and it causes endless problems.

So many of us respond to others with great compassion when they tell us something that they are ashamed of, or a strange thought they had. We are usually accepting and forgiving of them. Yet then we turn around and beat ourselves up for having the same thoughts! Why can we accept others' strange thoughts but not embrace our own? Are we to be held to some higher standard? Perhaps instead we can find a way to extend compassion to our own thinking.

It is like standing on the side of the road and watching cars go by. The cars are your thoughts. Sometimes you get in one and it takes you down the road a bit. Sometimes it drives you for hours, and you are swept away by your thinking. Yet you can always get out of the car and stand peacefully again by the side of the road to watch your thoughts go by.

Andrea, what I am proposing is that instead of being critical, be kinder toward your thoughts. Consider, as the Buddhists do, that we have a component of our mind that jumps all over the place. They call it the monkey mind. It has all sorts of random thoughts all the time. You don't need to be led around by those thoughts. Instead, you might regard your thoughts with some humor. If you are sad, could you comfort yourself with inner words of love and affection? Real self-care is an ongoing practice of being more compassionate to who you are as a person.

Maybe in our next role play, I will play the critical inner voice—the harsh coach. You could play the supportive, compassionate voice of lovingkindness: a voice which is tender and considerate. You might be able to reassure the coach that you are doing your best, and that is what's important. You might let her know that you will still win the game. You might even get her to loosen up. Then you could extend this warmth toward the rest of you, which desperately needs to hear loving words of encouragement. This change of tone in the inner ecology of your being can make all the difference.

Fondly yours,
David

PART II

Looking Back

A GOOD PORTION of the work of therapy is looking back at our childhoods and making sense of how early experiences shape who we are today. People worry that in therapy we are going to blame their parents, or that we might excuse all current personal responsibility and pin their problems on something that happened during childhood. That is the furthest thing from what good therapy does. Rather than ascribing today's ills to previous wounds, the work today is to better understand how early incidents formed how we see ourselves and experience the world.

Some of this work takes time, as there is a bit of digging through old experiences that needs to happen. We tend to bury painful memories and not recognize how they shape us. Like a young tree that is bent, but then adapts and grows strong around its bend, our minds tend to develop around neglectful or abusive experiences. It is a process to unearth these experiences and understand how they shape us, but going there typically proves quite valuable.

Our mind has two aspects, one that has new experiences, and the other that makes sense of those experiences. When we are young, we are constantly yearning to have new experiences. We are not focused as much on understanding them. As a result, early experiences get stored away deep within us without being processed. As we get older, we might turn back to those early experiences and start making sense of them. This is a brave process and one that often causes discomfort; but there is ultimately treasure in seeking to reconnect with lost aspects of who we are.

These letters address a few clients whose childhoods had a particular impact on how they live their current lives. In each letter I gently encourage them to go back to the past and look more closely at how their childhoods shaped them. In each case, I encourage them to undo past wounds and reach back to their childhood to find healing. The goal is for them to give to themselves that which they did not receive while growing up. If they did not have safety, then their job as adults is to create a safe world for themselves. If they were neglected, then their job is to better attend to their needs.

The point is not to blame our caregivers, but rather to stop perpetuating any imbalances that they may have caused. If we were raised by humans, then we were likely let down in some way. This seems to be part of the design. Our parents and caregivers do the best they can with the awareness they have, and then we are left to heal and make sense of it before we pass along anything to our children. Looking back and doing some healing helps with this transmission process. It allows us to treat ourselves and others more consciously.

Dear Olivia: The Powerful Effects of Neglect

Dear Olivia,

I received your email asking for my suggestions on how to handle a recent interaction with your ex-boyfriend. I know how troubling and confusing it can be when you have to interact with him. I see how it pains you. Relationships can bring us a lot of joy, but they are often the source of our pain. We long for companionship but also struggle when we are close with others. There are certainly strategies you might find helpful in your search for love; yet the deeper work that needs to be done is to look at how you often completely lose yourself in relationships.

We have been working on those times that you let others' opinions, impressions, interpretations, and beliefs completely shape who you are. I know it's painful to look at how you do this, how you almost become "de-selfed" in the face of others' reaction to you. While I get it that you would rather talk about how to navigate your dating life, I think the real work lies in how you respond when others neglect you. It is not easy to look at, but I believe that this is where the gold is.

We are social creatures. Our minds are set up to receive mirrored impressions from others, which then shape our sense of self. Our brains are wired to take in other people's reactions to us, and then modify how we express ourselves to curry favorable responses. This is just how we are. We seek out other people's validation. We can't help but do it.

Yet for healthy relationships to occur, we also need a wellspring of fortitude inside of us that boldly declares who we are. We need some sort of discernment so that we know who we are independent of others. When someone tells us it is black when we know it is white, we must be able to stick with our perceptions. When others neglect us, we can't crumble.

If the man you are dating is not interested, he does not get to become the authority on your worth. You must find a way to discern the sting of rejection from the truth of who you are. My concern is that if he accepts you, then you will feel valued; if he does not, then you will feel worthless. What a dangerous game to play with your heart!

My questions to you are: How can you know your worth apart from romantic relationships? How can you stand in the truth of who you are even in the face of someone else's neglect? Because if we know one thing, it is that people are fickle. They will vacillate. They will love you, then they will be preoccupied. If your sense of self rises and falls on their attention, then it is going to hurt badly when they can't attend to you.

My hope is that you can look more deeply at how you respond when people neglect you. For instance, when I was 10 minutes late to our session, you smiled and acted as if it didn't matter. You even apologized for calling and leaving a message to check if we were indeed having a session. It was my fault that I was late. It was unintentionally neglectful on my part. I would want us to talk more honestly about how that felt, because it would be okay with me if you felt hurt. It would be okay with me if you demanded that I be prompt at our sessions. Yet you did not say very much. We just moved on into our work, and it was business as usual. I worry that it was "neglect as usual."

Our interaction was just a microcosm of how your relationships go. Other people get away with neglecting you. I believe this stems back to how you were raised. Though your single mother was a kind and loving person, she neglected your needs and did not convey to you your proper worth and value. She made sure you had the basics but was not able to prioritize your emotional needs. She had her own struggles, and those took precedence. You became used to forfeiting your needs in the pursuit of her love and attention.

I know it is not easy to look back, but this is where some of the powerful effects of neglect were born. We are not looking to blame your mother, or to say that your childhood caused all of your current problems; we are instead aiming to understand where this "de-selfing" behavior originates so that we might get it out by the roots.

If someone, such as a boss or boyfriend, neglects you today, you have ways of dealing with it. You can try to fend off their disregard, or ignore their negligence. You can find ways of remedying their inattention by scheduling meetings or dates. Yet when you were a child, you did not have those resources. A child feels helpless when their needs are forsaken. It can feel like real abandonment when parents do not have time for you. They are our everything, and we will contort ourselves in order to find a way to feel loved.

I believe, Olivia, that you learned to lose yourself, and sacrifice your own needs, in order to feel loved while growing up. This has carried through to today. You make excuses for people who treat you poorly. You let their needs drive the relationship rather than advocating for yourself. We need to look back and tell that child that she is worthy. Her needs matter. No longer do you need to make excuses for others. It is okay to demand the best from them. Some people will indeed rise to this challenge.

To get there you need to remember your true worth. It is not determined by how others view you. That is just outsourcing your well-being to others rather than generating your sense of self from within. You determine who you are. Your work, on a day to day ongoing basis, is to live your life in ways that honor, value, and acknowledge who you are. How you do that is entirely up to you!

Fondly yours,
David

Dear Mary,

I am watching you run your marriage into the ground. I can't stop you, and you know I can't stop you. I think you know that you are running your marriage into the ground, and I believe that you don't want to stop it.

I am watching you flame out in your career, too. I can't stop you from getting yourself fired, and I don't think you want me to stop you. Yet you come in each week and tell me provocative and painful stories of how everything in your life is falling apart.

I don't know if you want me to feel sorry for you, to lament with you, to help you see how you are creating this situation, or to help you better understand why it's happening. As a matter of fact, I don't think you want me to do any of these things. You have actually told me that you don't want any of that from me. Years of psychoanalysis have made you way too savvy for any of my basic interventions. Instead, I think that you want me to watch with you as you blow up your marriage and get canned at work.

I am supposed to sit with you as you purposefully destroy what you have created. I guess I could do that if you want. It is painful and a bit curious to me why you would want to do this to yourself, or have me witness it, but you keep telling me that it is what you want. You are not interested in my interpretations or my sympathy. You clearly see how you are causing these circumstances, so any sort of behavioral intervention on my part would have little merit. So each week you regale me with colorful accounts of your spouse's latest disappointing actions or your boss's oppressive tactics, and how you masterfully did the exact thing that would exacerbate the situation.

You know, Mary, the funny thing is that I really like you. I look forward to our meetings. Your mind moves so fast and I enjoy the endless references you weave into the vivid tales of your pending demise. I am not usually a fan of sarcasm, but your self-effacing wit, combined with your special brand of snark, is quite enlivening. If you weren't in so much pain, it seems that you would truly be amused by it all.

There are times when you will pause your stream of self-flagellation, and your brilliance will emerge. These are the moments that I love, when you catch yourself, and the impact of your own words hit you deeply. Last week you stopped for a long while after you casually said, "You can't replace that which was never there." I didn't know what you meant, and it seemed at first as if you didn't either.

"What was never there?" I asked.

"Care," you said, "a basic care from my parents when I was fifteen. They had so much else going on in their lives that they really didn't pay me too much attention. My father's career was everything to him. He was always traveling. Even though my mother was there physically, she was too depressed to really be present in any meaningful way. I felt like I was living alone."

I know this story. You've told it to me a number of times, but it bears repeating. Your father was hardly present in your life, and your mother's depression kept her bedridden quite often, leaving you to fend for yourself. Your aunt and uncle played a big role in raising you, but they were not as consistent as they could have been in order to meet your needs.

You can't replace what was never there. The basic love, attention, and tending to a child of 15 was not there. Making sure you had lunch, being on top of your homework, coming to your plays, listening to your friendship and dating stories—none of that happened. You didn't have any of that basic care. What struck you as tremendously ironic is that you have been trying in vain to replace the basic care that was supposed to be there, but which actually never was. It's an unfillable emptiness: a sort of phantom limb syndrome of your heart.

In your adult life you have been searching for care and love from your spouse, authority figures such as your boss, and from anyone who would be in a position to care. Yet any time they get close, the wound of loss and neglect reopens. Their love hits the emptiness and starvation of that 15-year-old that still lives within you. While we might imagine it would feel good to finally receive the care that you never received, instead it hurts. Like the response to blaring a spotlight into the eyes of someone who has lived in the dark, your response to someone caring is to recoil.

Perhaps now I know why you have been torching your life, and why you have been telling me all the gory details of acting angrily in work meetings, intentionally missing deadlines, picking fights with your spouse, and drinking yourself to sleep each night. You want me and others to know how much you suffered as a teenager. You want us to know what it was like to never have had that care. You want me in particular to understand the folly you experience trying to replace that which was never there.

I can already feel you rejecting this interpretation. Maybe it would be too painful for you if I got it right … too painful if anyone got it right, even yourself.

Perhaps you tell me about your self-destructive ways so that you can demonstrate how nobody can get it right, how trying to replace that which was never there is an impossible task. Yet you keep compulsively trying to fill the emptiness within you until it becomes pure comedy. If the choice is to laugh or cry, perhaps you are choosing to laugh. Whichever the case, there is a hole within you. Maybe if you stopped trying to fill it, you would be able to accept all the good things in your life. I know that there are pains from the past, but you are really a good person, and have created a good life. My hope is that little by little you will let the goodness in, and that you will start taking in the care and affection which you so deeply deserve.

Fondly yours,
David

Dear Roni,

You work so hard. Both in life and in therapy, you try to get things right, and you often succeed. The effort you put into figuring yourself out and making things function in your life is very inspiring. Nobody would fault you for resting on your laurels.

Try as you might, however, you are as stuck as when you first came into therapy over two years ago. You report being just as anxious, that your friendships still feel one-sided, that your relationship with your mother is just as cold and distant. Just last week you reported having another incident in which you froze up and had to leave a work meeting, only to burst into nonstop tears in the bathroom.

Why does this keep happening despite your tremendous dedication to your psychological development? You come faithfully to our weekly meetings, always on time. You've been journaling, reading additional self-help books, and have deepened your yoga practice. Yet why haven't we broken through to make any real difference with your anxiety?

I wonder if your maladaptive solutions are getting in the way. Maladaptive solutions are unhealthy methods that we have developed, often when we were younger, to solve particularly troubling problems. We find ways of solving the problem, yet the solution ends up causing more issues than the original problem did in the first place. Maladaptive solutions are a type of overcompensation that help for a while, yet just get us more stuck.

For instance, if you have a bad back that makes it difficult to pick up heavy objects, you might start using your shoulders more to lift. Over and over you use your shoulders until you start to feel strain, until one day you tear a ligament in your rotator cuff. This leaves you in quite a bit of pain, so you go to the doctor who tells you that you can't use your shoulder for six weeks until it heals. Now you can't lift anything! What started as a bad back has become a torn ligament in your shoulder, leaving you unable to do any heavy lifting at all.

Using your shoulders to compensate for your bad back could be considered a maladaptive solution. Instead of getting to the root issue and strengthening your back, you do what most of us do. You go for the readily available, easy fix. You develop a strong suit, in this case your shoulders, and rely on that to get you through whatever the issue is at hand.

Psychologically speaking, when people come to therapy, they often come in complaining about a maladaptive solution that has started to cause them pain. They want help with anger management, for instance, yet the real issue is their unresolved grief about a recent loss. They want to solve the shoulder injury, not realizing they still need to strengthen their back. For you, Roni, your maladaptive solution may have been the ability to hold in your feelings and put on a good face. You've been able to adopt a pleasant and pleasing disposition even when you feel upset. When you talk about what it was like in your home growing up, around 12 or 13 years old, it makes sense that you weren't able to express your feelings. It was too chaotic at home, and it benefitted you to cut off emotionally and please those around you. It was, in fact, a useful solution at the time. However, now I believe that the emotional cutoff is causing you more problems than the original issue it was solving.

Today, your pleasant and pleasing behaviors keep you stuck in unsatisfying relationships. It is difficult for you to be genuine with others, and for others to get close to you. This is not because there is anything inherently wrong with you; rather, it is that you have been employing this old, outworn, maladaptive solution of pretending to be pleasant. My sense is that when you feel anxious, it is because your real feelings, deep down, start to stir. Since you have cut yourself off from them, the feelings register as anxiety and you do what you can to stuff them down even more.

We need to find another way! We need to safely make room for you to feel the feelings rather than to block them out. If you start to do that, Roni, my hunch is that you will begin to find relief from your anxiety. Little by little we can revisit those old feelings that have been repressed since you were 12 or 13 years old. There is a lot to uncover but just like strengthening the back instead of just fixing the injured shoulder, we need to get to the root of the issue.

Getting to the root might not feel so good at first, but over time I believe that it will bring you great relief. At the very least we could dial back the level at which you employ your maladaptive solution. You could ramp down those behaviors just a bit and see what happens. My sense, from what you tell me, is that your maladaptive solutions make it difficult for others to trust you. I bet they sense that you are not being authentic with them. They may worry that if you have a strong feeling around them, you won't be real about it. They might not know what is really going on with you. This leaves them on shaky ground and they move away from you.

This is not your fault. You are just employing an old relational pattern to keep yourself safe. It worked at age 12, but now it is having the opposite effect as an adult. I remember the story you told me a year ago about your ex-boyfriend. You were having strong feelings about something hurtful he said to you, but you did not do anything about it. You knew you were unhappy and felt uncared for, but you quickly stuffed down those feelings in favor of acting as if you were fine. Do you remember how he responded? He freaked out because he could tell that you were not being genuine with him. When you eventually burst into nonstop weeping a day later, he got scared and ran for the hills! This left you feeling even more rejected and reinforced a belief that you need to stuff down your feelings.

This is an example of how your maladaptive solution pushed him away. He ran because you weren't being honest, not because you had expressed your feelings.

No amount of therapy, journaling, reading, or yoga is going to unlock a new insight. Instead we need to do the deeper work of dialing down your maladaptive solutions and allowing for more authentic expression. This is slower, harder work, but I believe that this is where the treasure is. This is where you will find relief from anxiety, and more satisfaction in your relationships. It will be like shedding the old, outworn layers of who you were, and returning to who you truly are. I can't wait to get to know who that is.

Fondly yours,
David

Dear Aaron,

For the last few days I have been thinking about your story from when you were 16. I can see in my mind's eye that impressionable little guy, trying to be tough, yet so vulnerable to what his father was saying to him. He wanted to be his own man, but he was too young to stand up on his own. My heart really goes out to that younger version of you. He is with you today perhaps more than you realize.

Sometimes when I am working with an individual, I feel like I am working with more than one person. In your case, Aaron, it often feels like I am talking to the adult 45-year-old man as well as the 16-year-old boy. There are times when what you say, even the way you talk, sounds like an adolescent talking. The self-conscious way in which you see yourself, and how you think about the world, sometimes come from this stuck, regressed 16-year-old part of you. In psychological terms, we would call this arrested development. Aspects of you are frozen, beyond space and time, in the form of the 16-year-old.

Now, this is obviously a mental construct. The inner adolescent is a portal to an entire collection of thoughts, feelings, and reaction formations that shape you. When your father told you what a failure you were because you got a D in Algebra, and when he rudely expressed his disappointment when you didn't make the school basketball team, the younger you must have made some sort of interpretation. He must have felt there was indeed something deeply wrong with him. Why would his father say all these things otherwise?

You were not developed enough to know that your father was simply acting out his own undeveloped teenage parts that never received the love and acceptance from his own parents. Perhaps now as an adult you see that more clearly. Yet as a teenager yourself back then, you couldn't have known that your father's rage was more about him than it was anything about you. Year after year of his rejection has caused you to deeply believe that there is something wrong with you, and that you are weak. He thought his tough love would make you strong, but instead it created a deep chasm of self-blame and loathing that still has you in its grip today.

Presently, you find yourself underemployed at a retail job, with a spouse who is pressuring you to find better work. You were told while growing up that you should succeed in school and that being a successful professional is the most important goal. Anything other than academic and professional success would be beneath you. Though you have tried making a go of it in real estate, you know it is not where your interests lie. You have not done very well in your industry because it really does not suit your abilities. You have set yourself up for more failure by trying to follow in your father's footsteps. It has been a painful journey for that sweet 16-year-old.

I want to reach you and end this faulty belief system that says that there is something wrong with you. I want to help you release the lies you have been telling yourself—the ones that say you are a failure. Yet there is only so much I can do. I can talk with the 45-year-old man and try to get the message through, but I can only go so far. I could tell the 16-year-old that he is not a failure, that he is interesting and intelligent, that he has demonstrated tremendous strength, and that his worth is not determined by his achievements, but by just being who he is. Yet if you are still telling him he is a failure and pointing out each and every flaw, then my words will only do so much.

You have to be the one to heal that 16-year-old inside. You would have to start seeing his bravery and abilities rather than continuing to point out his shortcomings. In a funny way, Aaron, you are parenting the younger you similarly to how your father did. You are perpetuating the messages that he ingrained in you. This is such a common thing. Our parents send us particular messages in our childhood and then we carry the torch into adulthood.

I think of our childhood brains as something like silly putty. Do you remember that toy? Usually the first thing we do with silly putty is to press it against newspaper. Remarkably it holds an imprint of that image. When we are young, our brains are as impressionable as the putty. Early experiences leave an indelible mark that we carry with us into life. As we age, our brains become less easily impacted. We can have reparative experiences, but those early messages get in there, often pre-verbally, and lay a foundation for our sense of self.

Do you remember how to get rid of those newspaper imprints? You would just stretch and smush the putty until the image disappeared. You could roll it into a ball and then flatten it out again as a blank canvas for the next image. The same can be done for our minds. We can metaphorically go back to the life of the 16-year-old and stretch, smush, and roll him into a ball so that the faulty imprints are removed. Just like the silly putty, he will be less shiny than he was right out of the box, but we can help him be free from the past. In a way, our work is to bring him out of the past into your present life where you might care for him.

I ask you, Aaron, what do you want to say now to the wounded 16-year-old? What are the words he needs to hear from you that he never got to hear growing up? Can you tell him how valuable and worthwhile he is? Would you be willing to go toward and be with his past wounds? Perhaps as you get to know him, you might even find what he really loves. You might find his hidden joy, passion, and enthusiasm for life.

While you have been stuck as an adult to find what you truly love, your teenage self knows exactly where his passions lie. He holds the key to finding your lost love and power in this world. Getting back in touch with him, and attending to his old hurts, is not easy but it might just be the answer. It might feel like going back into the hell of childhood and reliving the pain. However, our work is a rescue mission to retrieve the lost joys of childhood that you left behind. I am on this mission with you, and my sense is that we will not only find what you love, we may also find renewed purpose in your life today.

Fondly yours,
David

PART III

Needed Healing

MOST OF US THINK that there is something wrong with us. We think that we are the only one who feels a particular feeling, or has a weird set of thoughts and behaviors. Ironically, each of us believes that we are the strange one. We assume that there is something wrong with us. We each think that we are crazy.

The worst part of this is that this belief system factors into our self-concept. We start to identify with our quirks and make distorted interpretations about who we are. Painful past experiences cause wounds with which we start to identify. Shame takes over, and keeps us locked in a sense that we are crazy. People start to feel like they are horrible. How else could they explain why they do harmful things, or behave in unhealthy ways? They assume the worst and figure that they are bad. They form a sense of self that identifies around these distortions. Disavowals such as "I am messed up" or "I am weird" take over.

From meeting with countless people, I have come to see that any sense of being messed up or weird is simply an aspect of the human condition. We all have difficult thoughts and feelings. A lot of the work in therapy is to undo these distortions and to start living in our truth. My goal is to try to reach people and let them know that they are not strange, but are, in fact, part of a great, complex constellation of humanity. Getting this message past years of false interpretations, and faulty self-concepts, takes patience and insistence.

These next letters aim to bring unyielding healing to people who are stuck in thinking that there is something wrong with them. Rather than therapy helping them simply to change their behaviors, or giving them advice, they need to heal from painful self-concepts. They need to start seeing that they are perfectly okay as they are. They are lovable just being themselves. Often this is a difficult message for them to absorb through the false beliefs about their worth. Yet once they start to open up to the fact that there is nothing wrong with them, then needed healing can begin.

Dear Jessica: You Are Not Crazy

Dear Jessica,

I wish you could hear from other people as to what they are going through. They would tell you about their insecurities and petty behavior, their defensiveness, and critical inner voices. They would relate humiliating stories of how they bumble through their relationships, and push away the people they love. If you could just get on the inside of what occurs in other people's hearts and minds, I think you would find great relief.

You believe that you are the only one who has the thoughts you do, the feelings that overwhelm you, and the distorted self-perceptions that plague you. You think that there is something wrong with you; yet I reckon that if you heard from countless other people, from all walks of life, then you would start to see that the only thing wrong with you is that you are human.

Being a therapist, I have had the privilege of being on the inside of thousands of people's lives. I hear all sorts of stories. I listen as people share their innermost taboo thoughts and feelings. Sometimes it is a confession of sort, with people saying, "I've never told anyone this before." After many years of doing this, I have come to realize that the thoughts and feelings that we think are weirdly ours are simply part of the human condition. We are all strange somehow, yet we just don't share it with one another.

You grew up in a family where there was not much interest in one another's internal worlds. You were essentially told to keep your thoughts and feelings to yourself. Since nobody around you was talking about what was happening inside of them, you must have assumed that you were the only one who was having wild imaginations, scary dreams, obsessive thoughts, and outrageous fantasies. That assumption has followed you into adulthood. You still think you are weird for being how you are. No matter how many times I try to normalize what you are going through, it doesn't stand a chance in the face of your deep conviction that you are crazy.

Well, I am here to tell you that there is nothing wrong with you. In fact, you are deeply and wonderfully human. You are made up of the full range of human emotions, from joy to jealousy, from cruelty to wonderment. You are of the light and have a shadow, as do the rest of us. The trouble is that a lot of us are inauthentic with one another. We act as if we have it together, and we don't let on that we are overwhelmed.

Being one way and acting another is just our way of protecting ourselves. We are afraid that if others know what is really going on inside that *they* would think we are crazy and probably leave us. However, I believe the opposite is true. It is precisely our frailty, our humanness, which endears us to one another. You love the people in your life not because they are perfect, but because of their charming flaws.

In your family, the emphasis was on looking good. It was not just physically looking good but seeming smart, or having it together, or not being emotionally messy. It was not okay to say, "I can't figure this out," or "I'm scared. Can you help me?" Your family did not value their inner lives, and didn't teach you how to share your feelings.

With sharing feelings, there are three essential components. First we need to be able to feel our feelings. We need to be able to sit with them for a bit and let them move through us. Then we must look within to identify those feelings. We need to find words for what is happening. For example, "My stomach feels shaky. It's all in knots. I'm anxious." Then, to relate more deeply with others, we need to express those feelings with words. We might say, "I have a big presentation this afternoon. I'm anxious about it. That's why I'm not talking very much this morning." It's not too difficult a process once you get used to it, but when families are conditioned not to feel, not to identify, and not to express emotions, then it can be very crazy making indeed.

To your credit, Jessica, you have taken the steps to feel, identify, and express what is inside of you. You have reversed some of the conditioning that tells you to hold back what you really think and feel. You have become more sincere in your relationships and have let others see who you really are, even if it doesn't look so good that day. What is left is for you to realize that you are not weird or wrong for being the way that you are.

One reason I love group therapy is that you get to hear what is really going on in the hearts and minds of the other group members. One of the curative factors of groups is the recognition that you are not the only one who is having a particular experience. Though I understand that you are not ready to join a group right now, someday I would like you to have the firsthand experience of what really transpires within others. Like I said, I think this will give you great relief.

In the meantime, I encourage you to keep putting yourself out there in the right moments. When you sense that others are listening deeply, you might try sharing from a deeper place within. You may be surprised. The other person may relate that they also thought they were the only one who felt that way. They might have thought they were crazy as well. You could then tell them just how wrong they are!

Fondly yours,
David

Dear Terry: Well, Maybe You Are a Little Crazy

Dear Terry,

We don't have to stick to a script. There are a million ways to go, and even though your life may not be a cookie-cutter version of those around you, there is tremendous value in who you are. When others zig, you zag, and that is perfectly okay. In fact all of your differences and quirks are part of your charm. What got you teased on the playground in childhood makes you interesting as an adult. Your craziness is part of your uniqueness.

Being a little crazy can be a good thing sometimes. You have had experiences in life that are out of the norm (and out of this world), and it would be disingenuous for you to pretend that you are just like everyone else. You are who you are, and being true to yourself can make all the difference. It allows for more authentic relationships and reduces any sense of regret that might arise from trying to be someone you are not.

I know you have been in quite a lot of pain from taking the road less traveled. It is a solitary path in and of itself, and I know you have felt lonely. Your work as a travel writer makes your day to day quite different from those who have 9-to-5 jobs. You are single, don't want children, and are more interested in philosophy and nature than family and sports. Yet having interpreted your differences as craziness has made it even more difficult for you. Just because your life looks considerably different from that of your peers does not mean there is anything wrong with you. In fact your differences just might be the thing that adds value to this world.

We need more innovators, rule breakers, trailblazers, and mystics. Those who have been deemed crazy by the masses have been the ones who have changed the world for the better. Einstein is famously quoted as saying, "Great spirits have always encountered violent opposition from mediocre minds." If you are marching to the beat of your own drum, then you are assured to face reaction, criticism, and invalidation from others who can't understand you. Those who do not see what you have been through are sure to reject any expression of your deepest experiences. At best it will confuse them, at worst scare them.

So then, how are you to be yourself when others may not allow or accept your truth? First, you need to honor the validity of your own experiences. Almost everyone questions themselves, and thinks there is something wrong with them. It is even more seductive to indulge in this line of thinking when the world around you tells you that you look different, that your thinking is wrong, that you shouldn't feel what you feel, and that your fringe experiences are made up. To find the strength to be yourself in a conformist world, you most certainly need to honor that what you are going through in this life is valid. Instead of thinking you are crazy, know instead that it is precisely just that bit of craziness that enables you to do great things. This belief in yourself will be the definitive element of who you become.

To own your craziness while not becoming unglued is the key to juicy living. I am with you on the edges of what life may have to offer. I welcome your gentle exploration against the norms and into the unknown. Your interest in abstract philosophy, in the different way that cultures live, and in how people celebrate various rituals around the world makes you an explorer. Instead of approaching life with a definitive sense of knowing, the road less traveled involves being open to wonder. It embraces the Socratic Paradox which says, "I know one thing: that I know nothing." Rather than being certain about how everything is in life, our challenge is to stay open to the unknown even in the face of a world which values definitive answers. To do so, you have to realize that there is nothing wrong if you are confused. It is okay if everything you have known does not fit anymore.

Terry, your search for new understanding is valid and admirable. It is brave to let go of a prescribed sense of reality and find your own answers. You have to be a little bit crazy to take that route, and I find it inspiring that you are following your sense of wonder. In a way, I see you emptying out that which you have already known. I see you letting go of the world that has filled you. In your emerging emptiness, I imagine you like a basin ready to be filled with wonder. It looks to me to be a fruitful path.

I can walk with you on your path for a while, but there are directions that you must go down alone, perhaps even into the metaphorical dark forest. I know that you have it in you to take this path step by step and hold yourself together. My hope is that someday you will return and share with us what you have learned. I will be waiting at the edge of that forest to greet you, and to listen to the stories of the wonders you have discovered. I won't judge you or your stories. I won't think that you are crazy. Well, maybe just a little!

Fondly yours,
David

Dear Harper: You Are Not a Horrible Person

Dear Harper,

You are not a horrible person. I know it feels that way right now, but you really are not as bad as you fear. Yes, you have done some hurtful things. You have been careless with others' hearts. From your own pain you have disregarded the needs of others to get what you felt you needed. Was this devastating for your loved ones? Did this crush almost all the trust they had in you? Have you humiliated yourself and those around you? I am afraid so, yet I know I am not the first to say you have.

You are not the first person to have an affair with your coworker, nor will you be last. I know that deep down you fear you actually are a horrendous person. You worry that left to your own devices, your tendencies will always gravitate toward selfishness, ruthlessness, and cruelty. You fear that who you really are is someone who is unloving. This great, generous, loving mother figure that we see in front of us is just a carefully constructed act. Who you really are is a scoundrel! That's the fear you have, and I see how, right now, you think that might actually be true. Yet I am here to tell you that you are not a horrible person.

Even if it is just semantics, the shift from being a "horrible person" to being "someone who has done something horrible" makes a big difference. For if you believe that you are a horrible person, you are suggesting that there is a deep flaw within your being that may never change. It suggests something akin to basic sin, like you are tainted with horribleness.

Even worse, it suggests that there is nothing you can do about it. If you are truly rotten, then that is how you always have been and always will be. The inquiry stops right there. All you can do is to hold back the rottenness so that it doesn't stink too badly. However, if you look at yourself as being someone who has done something horrible, who has cheated, then it suggests you had, and still have, free will. Being a woman of free will suggests that you have agency. You had, and still have, choice. You can choose to be loving or to be cruel. It is up to you.

I think the difficult part for you to look at is that you repeatedly chose to have this affair even when your husband suspected you were. You lied to him, and gratified your own urges at the expense of his well-being. Even in the face of the impact of your behavior, you kept choosing what you knew would be hurtful. That might be a more difficult truth to face than the faulty belief that you are somehow tainted. Finding out whether you are a good or bad person is not that compelling of an investigation to me. A more interesting exploration, I believe, is to look at *why* you made horrible choices. You are a regular person who made poor choices. Why? The answers to that question are more complex.

I think that if you are honest, you would acknowledge that you were not satisfied in your marriage, but felt obligated to stay. You felt disconnected for years, but didn't know what to do to make things better. You felt guilty that he was overwhelmed with his career and with raising your children with you. Your needs were not getting met, and you didn't know what else to do. The relationship with your coworker emerged out of the blue and you felt better than you have in years. It was hard for you to let go of that new-found connection, even though you knew you were hurting your spouse. Once you were found out, you tried to stop the affair, but it took many months to really put it to rest. To your credit, you eventually started to look at why you were acting how you were, and have since made some changes to be more honest and transparent.

Now you aren't acting nearly as horribly as you were before. Your guilt and shame have made sure you'll never do that again. Yet how far have you come in becoming the truest version of your most loving and expansive self? How much more can you do to bring the most joy to other people's lives?

Let us see if we can have your guilt and shame about your past actions not trap you in a backwards, self-condemning spiral, but instead lead you forward toward loving choices. Your story is not fully written. You make choices every day that impact those around you. Though you have to look in the eyes of the people you hurt, can you find the strength to stay open and love them? When they share their pain, hurt, or fear, can you find a way not to shut down? Can you keep the guilt and shame from overwhelming you, and instead make a positive choice in that moment?

Sometimes you ask me how you are supposed to respond when your husband expresses to you his frustration and pain. We come up with ways to best handle this and that situation. Yet in our planning, we subtly invalidate the fact that you know, deep in your heart, how to be loving. You know what would be the kindest thing to do. You know how to be creative in your relationships.

Are you a horrible person? No, of course not. Yet, on some level, I don't think that even matters. Maybe the right question is, are you being horrible right now? What about in the next, upcoming difficult encounter? Are you going to be horrible then, or be loving instead? The determination of your worth comes in your moment-to-moment interactions. Where you have a choice is how you will handle the next difficult argument. Instead of being racked with guilt and shame about the past, could you show up as the deeply loving woman that you are? Will the goodness of who you are come forth? Right now, it is your choice.

Fondly yours,
David

Dear Daniel,

I know how much you have been through. It has been a difficult road for you. Little by little over the years you have come to tell me more and more of your story. I have learned of the sexual and emotional abuse you had to endure growing up. You have told me about how systemically you were trained and conditioned to go along with despicable acts; acts that cost you your innocence. While I know it is your path, and that you found a way to handle what has come your way, my heart does ache for you.

The abuse you suffered as a child is really not fair. It should not have happened to you, and I am sorry you had to go through it. Your abuser was a trusted neighbor, and you were taken advantage of when you were only six years old. This went on for a few years, and your parents did not believe you when you finally tried to tell them what happened. You started acting out your pain, which then got you into more trouble growing up. The confusion that followed you into young adulthood caused you to be promiscuous and risky. You were trying to work through what happened when you were younger, but it caused you even more pain; your attempts to get back a piece of your lost self made things worse. Through repeating painful patterns, and trying to master power games, all of your efforts were in the spirit of healing, but created more damage instead. I don't fault you for any of that, or for the residual mess you created along the way. I know you were trying your best to figure things out.

I haven't found an easy way to bring forgiveness into our conversations because I don't want to sound like I'm invalidating your experiences. Yet I do want to help you find a way to forgive what happened. If you are still bitter and hurt about your abuse, then you can be bitter and hurt. I am not telling you to let go of those feelings. They serve you in some way. I am suggesting, however, that at some point we need to look at what it would take to forgive those who hurt you. You may benefit from exploring what forgiveness looks like, and I want to tell you why.

The power of forgiveness is that it allows you to be with what is. When something traumatic happens to us, our minds immediately go to work rationalizing what happened. We know that the abusive event should not have happened. We recognize that something has gone terribly wrong and we do whatever we can to remedy it. The downside to this sort of rationalizing is that we continue to live in a world that says, "This should not have happened," because really it shouldn't have. However, instead of living in a world that incorporates what did happen, we stay in a mindset of what *should* have been. I should have been protected. Those people should not have treated me the way they did. I should have known better. What would it be like had this not happened, and I had stayed intact?

Many of us remain in this alternate reality of what *should* or *could* have been for quite a long time. It is natural to do so. Yet at some point we may look at integrating what actually did happen into your understanding of who you are. Like a tree that has suffered from another tree falling on it, we must wind our way around the injury and keep stretching skywards. That injured tree is not as impressive as an unspoiled mighty oak reaching toward the heavens, yet it shows a certain willingness and character as it finds a way to keep growing. Those are the sort of peculiar trees, the ones wrapped around another fallen tree, or growing out of a rock, that people drive from miles around to catch a glimpse of. It is living with our woundedness that makes us remarkable.

Daniel, you don't have to forgive those who hurt you, now or ever. You really don't. Yet I want you to be aware of what happens when you do begin to forgive. When you allow for what actually did happen, you start to create your life again. When you accept your past, great internal resources are freed up that allow you to design your future. Just know that when you are being bitter about your past, you are not working on your future. I am not saying it is necessarily better to be working on your future than healing from your past. I am just making a case for being aware of which one you are doing.

I could imagine you saying, "Right now I'm thinking about my past and lamenting what happened. I'm angry and sad, and I want to stay in and take care of myself." That would be totally normal. I completely get that.

Yet know that when you say, "I want more satisfying relationships. I want to create a job that inspires me. I want to make a difference in the lives of others," you are up to the business of creating your future. You are not lamenting the past, but instead you are in the present, dreaming of what might be possible in your life. To do this, we need to find a way for you to incorporate what happened to you in the past, and accept that it is part of who you are now. By forgiving what happened, you claim a power that makes you more present in creating your life.

I worry that some of this may sound trite, that I am somehow telling you to move on. I don't want to suggest that at all. Instead I want to honor what happened to you, and help find a way for it to inform what you might create in your life. I hope for you the possibility of reclaiming what was lost, repairing what was broken, and realizing what might be possible. Forgiveness just might be the way to get there.

Fondly yours,
David

PART IV
Needed Advice

SOMETIMES PEOPLE COME TO THERAPY seeking advice. They want to find immediate answers to life's persistent questions. I see my job not as giving them advice, as my answers may not necessarily work for them. They don't always work even for me! Instead, I see the goal as helping them access their native wisdom and find their own answers. My job is to help remove whatever obstacles are blocking access to their own information.

If accessing our wisdom were easy, then people would figure out their problems right away. I would see them for one or two sessions. Yet it often takes time. Perfectly intelligent people come to therapy looking for advice because they can't always see their issues clearly. It exists in their blind spots. My role is to help gently illuminate those blind spots so that they can start seeing more clearly, and use their own wisdom to solve problems. Sometimes this illumination takes the shape of telling stories, relating my own experiences, or sharing alternate possibilities they might consider.

However, sometimes people just need someone to tell it to them straight. They want good old advice, and appreciate direct feedback. I usually find something to say by sifting through what the client has shared with me, and reflecting it back to them. The answers are usually in what people say if we but listen closely. Yet even with all the analysis and exploration, sometimes people just need a gentle nudge in the right direction.

The letters that follow are to clients who are bright and intelligent. Yet even in their brilliance they are stuck in old patterns. They just need a little encouragement to get moving again in the direction they are already heading. While some of my language is direct, it comes from a place of compassion and understanding. While the client might feel a bit challenged, my hope is that straight talk will lead to bringing out their best. As I say in one of the following letters, "As your therapist, if I can't tell it to you straight, then who can?"

Dear Cindy: Less Is More

Dear Cindy,

There is so much of you! You come into sessions smiling, warm, greeting me with energy and positivity. You get right down to work. Sometimes you roll in with the tears right there under the surface, ready to flow. Once they do, your lightning-quick mind gets right to work on your inner processes. Before we know it, you have new insights and move into new dimensions of who you are. It takes a quick mind and an open heart to keep up with you and hold the space.

You are on full tilt at all times, and it works. You have created a life filled with so many good things. You report a flow in your life, and that people gravitate to you. Yet we are seeing in our work together that there are some side effects to being "on" all the time. You respond to the demands of others at a moment's notice but abandon your own projects. You sacrifice time for you in order to pour yourself into the various projects for which you have signed up.

This is all a part of having a big life, yet we are starting to see that you can't run full steam ahead all the time. Your health is suffering as a result. The physical symptoms are telling you to slow down. You are learning the hard way that sometimes less is more.

If we are always giving our gifts, then sometimes they float away like water without the glass. I do not do therapy with people I meet at cocktail parties. I am not healing people who sit next to me on the bus. Sure, I am pleasant and friendly; but only when the moment is right, when it is time for me to work, do I try to give the gift of healing and deep listening to others.

Harnessing what you have to offer might make a huge difference for you. You don't have to help and heal others everywhere you go. You could have permission to dial down to partially open: to run at 50, even 20, percent of your capacity. This sort of pacing, or self-management, might allow you to feel more cared for, to feel valued for you just being you.

The epitome of this was when you were at your sister's wedding, and instead of enjoying the experience in the wedding party, you spent most of the time helping the caterers who were short-handed, and then listening to the sob story of your cousin who had just broken up with her boyfriend. Everyone appreciated you helping the caterers, and your cousin gushed over how wonderful it was of you to listen to her, yet you reported feeling pretty drained by the end of the event. You did so much for everyone else and didn't take time to enjoy the moment for yourself.

Somewhere along the way in life you may have felt more valued by how much you do for others, rather than just being you. We can receive a lot of validation when we give to others. They tell us how wonderful we are, and how they can't do it without us. That reinforces us to keep giving and giving. These are all good things; that is, they are good until we over-identify with being a giver. Then we end up not being okay with ourselves unless we are giving.

It feels to me like you might be attached to being on all the time. I wonder how you would feel to take on a "less is more" approach and hold back at times. It might feel strange to let others take care of things. You might even wonder what your value is if you aren't the one running the show.

Yet my hope is that you will feel relief, and rest … and that you will know more deeply that you are beloved not for all that you do, but for simply who you are.

Fondly yours,
David

Dear Zach: Get Off Your Phone

Dear Zach,

Thank you for sharing with me today your dreams and plans for the future. I don't know exactly how we got on the topic of your 5-, 10-, and 20-year plans for your life, but to hear you talk about what you plan to create, I have to admit I am quite inspired.

In meeting with you for the last few months, I did not know you had that much going on inside of you. Your more reserved presentation does not let on how much ambition and passion you possess. The vision you have for your future, running a nonprofit that helps bring healthy foods to America's food deserts, I imagine would bring you great satisfaction, and would touch the lives of many others. I can see you being up to all sorts of great things on a daily basis, and how full your day-to-day life would be.

You just need to get off your phone first!

You have great dreams, but your days are spent on your phone, or by playing video games. On a daily basis you don't seem to be up to much aside from carving out time to be online. I don't mean this as a criticism; rather, it is more as a statement of fact. You yourself report that most of your waking hours are spent in front of a screen. I really don't have a problem with that, yet this way of living doesn't jive with everything you expressed today about your future. If you are going to live big, then you will have to get *into* your life.

You see, most of us are not really *in* our lives. Most of us hang out on the sidelines and act as if we are up to a lot. When we root for our favorite sports team, we say, "We won!" Yet we really did not do much. We sat in the stands and watched as the players won. They had the experience. We were on the sidelines. Any athlete, musician, actor, or performer will tell you that to be on the field, on the stage, is entirely different from watching.

The highs are higher and the lows are lower when we are "on the field" of our lives. There are much bigger risks when we put ourselves out there. We could be rejected. We might fail. We likely will get hurt. Yet I think those are the moments that we remember most: when we went for it … when we played big.

Zach, I don't want to play you small. As your therapist, if I can't tell it to you straight, then who can? I see you today as someone who is on the sidelines of your life. You have great ideas but do not take steps toward making them happen. You long for a relationship but don't put yourself out there to meet new people. You have great ideas for the nonprofit, but you spend most of your time on your phone.

I ask then, what keeps you from being more active in your life? Why aren't you interacting face to face with others more? Why has it taken me so long to get to know you? I think the answers have to do with confidence. Your lack of clarity about who you are keeps you from feeling confident enough to engage more fully in life. I see your phone and the video games as a way of coping with this lack of confidence. It is a way of self-soothing, and it allows you to feel engaged and competent without having to take real-life risks. The phone is not the problem; your confidence level is.

I want to help you find your unique voice. I want us to find the deep gift inside you that you have to give to the world. I think you will find great joy when you bring it out. Yet what I hear from you is that you are easily stymied when someone disagrees or disapproves of you. Your sense of self crumbles easily in the face of their judgment. You try to blend in and conform to the norms of your peers. I know this doesn't feel good, so I hope we can work to get you stronger and clearer about who you are. For if you are confident, I can see you taking the needed risks to create the life you want.

Make no mistake about it, if you are going to go big in your life, then there will be some obstacles. There will be missteps and also criticisms from others. Yet when the time comes to stop playing it safe, when you build up a sense of confidence enough, and when it hurts more to hold back than it does to go for it, then you will take the next step. When you realize that you have nothing to lose, then you will take the leap.

Perhaps you need to go yell into the wind, or maybe you should throw yourself into something unexpected. Get on a plane, train, or bus and travel somewhere new. Lose yourself in a long conversation late into the night, in person, with someone you care about. Take a long walk in the woods. Whatever it is, find a way to get out of your own way: out of your head, past your comfort zone, into your body. Dive back into your life and find confidence in who you are. As you do, I see great days ahead for you. I can't wait!

Fondly yours,
David

Dear Malcolm,

I wish things for you. I don't sit back and watch to see how you're going to figure things out, just to say, "Oh well," when it doesn't go your way. I deeply wish for your well-being. I deeply long to see you triumph and to be your best!

Here you are, a painter with a unique talent, yet you toil away at your stressful job. There is no room for your art when you are filled every day with stress and demands. An artist needs a silence in which to paint, and you need an empty space in order to step more fully into your life. You need to empty out! Yet you have spent decades filling in the emptiness.

You have filled it with toxic relationships, sex, food, drinking, anything to escape from yourself and your emptiness. Now, ironically, you are looking for some emptiness, some quiet from all the chaos you have created, and goodness knows you need it! The only way I can see for you to get away from the stressful day to day is to stop working, and to devote yourself to your art. You need to get into the studio more frequently, so that you can live out some of your dreams!

I am constantly thinking about how I can help you get there. I have been starting with letting you know that you are not alone. First, when we meet, I am totally with you. I try to convey to you how I get what you are going through, even if my life looks different. I try to let you know that as a man, I can relate to your struggles. You are not the only one.

Second, I try to inspire you. I work like hell so that you find inspiration rather than be stopped by the numerous obstacles in your way. How much motivation do you need in order to overcome everything that you face in life? I want to help you find tremendous purpose and determination to overcome whatever you face.

Third, I try to create emptiness. You need time and space. You need some room within yourself so that you feel peaceful enough to create your art. If we could sit in silence together, perhaps that would be the most helpful thing for you, as you might have a chance to quiet your mind and let go.

How many past relationships do you hold onto? How many women fill the space in your heart and mind where artistic expression could exist? I know that it is hard to sit with the emptiness inside yourself. However, it is from this void that you have birthed some of your greatest work. From nothing something comes, and from within yourself you have created great art that has been meaningful for many admirers.

I wish for you to do something meaningful. I see how you glow when you do. I see how your spirit shines through when you bring your art into the world. That I can be a part of helping it get out of you into the world is a true honor.

I see how countless inconsequential distractions threaten your work. I see how you can get lost in the ordinariness of life. Yet you have something meaningful to do. You have a gift to give. It is birthed out of your pain, and while it is, of course, a good thing to soothe this pain, you risk losing your edge.

Stay edgy, my friend! I am here to help you through it.

Fondly yours,
David

Dear Paul: Be Willing to Gamble

Dear Paul,

You hold on so tightly. It is painful to watch you clinging. It is precisely this sort of clinging that brings us great suffering in life. There is nothing wrong with becoming attached. In fact, being attached to people, places, or experiences allows us to enjoy them even more. Sentimentality can be a lovely thing. Yet when life moves along, when people leave, places change, or experiences end, then holding onto the way it was will hold you back.

Clinging to what is no longer serving you is painful, but sometimes it feels like there are no other options. Right now you can't see what your life would be like if you let go of this relationship that you have been in for over five years but has grown distant and cold. Though the relationship no longer serves you, it feels like life and death when you talk about what it would be like to lose it. It is as if you won't be able to survive on the other side of a breakup. You are not alone. Most of us would rather cling to what is dead than take the leap into the void of the unknown.

Paul, we do not know what your life would be like on the other side of letting go of this relationship. It was really good for a while, but you have reported how toxic it has become. The emotional distance has increased and the two of you have started fighting with one another as a futile way of trying to reconnect. You've become shut down and resentful. You report it is a lot like how your father was when you were growing up. If you continue on this path, we know that you will likely end up a lot like your father: disconnected, frustrated, solitary. Yet if you let go of this relationship and take a risk to move into the unknown, then we don't really know who you will become. We might imagine who you will be, yet in a lot of ways it is difficult to see. If there is a chance that you will be happier, would you be willing to go for it? If you would become more fulfilled, live a healthier life, be stronger within, develop a better sense of your worth, and find a deeper, more fulfilling love, would you let go of the remnants of this relationship to which you cling?

Sometimes in life, we need to be willing to lose if there is a chance that we can gain. Even when there are no guarantees, can you heed the call to move along and jump into what might be next? There is a *chance* that you will be happier, more fulfilled, and stronger as a person if you let yourself do that. You may also end up feeling worse and realizing that this relationship was the best thing you will ever have. It is a gamble. Yet you can't gamble unless you are willing to lose.

It is really a question of how you want to live your life. What sort of person are you? Are you someone who will cling at all costs to what you know in order to avoid any disruptions? Or are you willing to gamble? Are you willing to roll the dice to see what comes next in your life?

As you know, Paul, I don't necessarily advocate living too far out on the edge. You might fall off if you do. Yet there are moments in life when it is time to risk losing what you have in favor of attaining something greater. To quote the ancient Chinese philosopher Lao Tzu, "When I let go of what I am, I become what I might be."[3]

It is a risk, this sort of letting go. Who you have been, Paul, has been pretty good. You've been connected and playful in this relationship. Letting go of it won't be easy. It will be a loss. I think that in his quote Lao Tzu was acknowledging the difficulty of letting go. You will no longer be who you are. Instead you invest in the possibility of who you might become. He is not saying, "I become what I *will* be." Instead he is referencing what you *might* be. He recognizes the gamble. He knows that there is no guarantee.

As a result of this uncertainty, most of us stay with what we know. We hold onto what we already have. We rest with who we already are. In gambling terms, we "stick" instead of "hit." Please know that when we stick in life, we get stuck.

Paul, you who clings to what has been, you run the risk of not becoming what you might be. If you could just glimpse what you might be, I think it may be easier for you to let go. What I see is the possibility of someone who can build a great confidence, strength, and a tremendous capacity to love. You are already a loving guy, but without your ability to know that you can make it on your own without this relationship, you let yourself slip into a complacency that, yes, might keep you safer, but might also erode you from the inside. I see way too many relationships that suffer from the corrosive effects of stagnation.

If you are willing to wager what you have for what might come, then I think you will find that even if you struggle, you will benefit from the process of being willing to evolve. It is precisely our unwillingness to let life grow us that causes suffering. Flowing along with change requires a certain grace. Even in the face of leaving the solid ground of what you have known and leaping into the unknown, trust that you will land again in something new, and hopefully better.

I can see a bit of where you are headed. It looks bright to me. Yet I cannot leap for you. You have to be the one who goes for it. You have to play the game and be willing to lose. I don't know what will happen, but I will be right there with you along the way as we find out.

Fondly yours,
David

PART V
Growing Pains

THE NITTY-GRITTY OF THERAPY happens when people really dig down into their core beliefs about who they are. This is when the adventure begins, and people's entrenched, hurting places start to move and shake. Often it is really uncomfortable when such psychological growing pains happen. When life brings us experiences that challenge our basic values and primary concepts of who we are, we are called to a crossroads. Do we continue down the same outworn path that we have known, or will we try something new?

Recent research is showing that talk therapy can alter brain activity.[4] The relationship with the therapist can change the way the brain fires. For instance, if people in a client's life respond the same way every time the client tells their story, then their brains are likely predicting that they will always get the same response. Yet if the therapist responds in a different way, perhaps with more compassion and understanding, then it might open up new pathways in the client's brain. At least it might open new possibilities to lift them from a well-worn rut of behavior.

In Hinduism, there is a name for this well-worn rut of behavior. It is called samskara. A samskara is a deep impact or imprint in the structure of our mind. The samskaric path is one that we repeat over and over, like a wagon wheel tracing the previous path. It feels familiar to put the wheel in the track and let life flow as predicted. Yet for one reason or another, these paths get disrupted, and it causes us tremendous distress. Sometimes an event in life will trigger the shift. A sudden loss or accident can cause people to question everything that they knew was real. Tremendous growing pains emerge when people are overwhelmed by these changes. Therapy is a great refuge for working through this sort of occurrence.

Yet it is also possible to preempt being triggered by life's events, and instead intentionally get out of the samskaric rut. When one is doing their own in-depth work, they can explore where there are imbalances and grow in new ways. When this opportunity arises in session, I try to go for the mark. I try to trigger the deeper growth so that it can be done proactively in the safety of therapy, rather than having life push us along.

Regardless of how these deeper changes emerge, they are often accompanied by great growing pains. The following letters address clients in the midst of growing pains. Their work is to look at some of their shadow material: the aspects of themselves from which they have long ago distanced. As I say to one of them, it is one thing to bring more light to the light, but another thing to illuminate the darkness in us.

Dear Louisa: Relax the Clench

Dear Louisa,

There is a part of you that is clenching really tightly. Shutting down, holding back, resisting, and grasping for dear life, this part of you needs to relax. It lies in your mind and could use a break. Yet I am finding it almost impossible to reach this part of you and help it relax because I also have this clench.

I try to see myself as someone who is open, compassionate, and inquisitive. When things are confusing, I try to stay available to new information and wisdom. I try to go with the flow. Like you, I consider my heart wide open; yet if we are both honest, we will see that in the corner of our psyche lie pieces of our mind and our emotions that are closed off. I call these pieces "The Clench."

When we take a deep breath we might notice The Clench. Our jaw may be pinched tightly, our shoulders slightly raised up to our ears, or our chest closed with our heart center shut down. These clenched parts are undeniable once we tune into them. Louisa, you are such a kindhearted person, but I would venture to say that a lot of your struggles and sadness come from being shut down and held back. I am not blaming you. In fact I am relating to The Clench. I've got it, too. The difference for you would be acknowledging that you have it rather than denying that it exists. Being honest about our resistance to life can actually help us feel more alive.

The Clench is there for a reason. It is the result of steeling ourselves against the winds of life. It has been our armor against the slings and arrows of being sensitive in a harsh world; we may have been hurt in a relationship or let down by various life circumstances. The Clench is usually upset. Or maybe yours is angry. Sometimes The Clench is afraid. Often it is uptight. Like any clench, it is the collection of the parts of us that are closed into a ball, squeezed together, and shut tightly.

Louisa, can you find this part of you that is closed like a fist? To throw a punch we must first clench our fist, and this aspect of you is threatened, defensive, and on edge. Since you are quite open hearted and loving, this part of you is subtle. Since you are generally at ease in the world, and secure in yourself, you might have to pay close attention to notice The Clench inside of yourself. There is beauty and love in you, yet our most impactful work has come when you have acknowledged the parts of you that are resistant to life and then have found a way to bring soothing relief.

It is one thing to bring more light to the light, but another thing to illuminate the darkness in us. When you have addressed that which is hurt inside you, your life benefits. I would encourage you to relax that which is clenched within you. Be tender with yourself and approach The Clench with compassion and TLC, just as you would anyone in your life who is shut down and closed off. Be patient, as emotional tightness is developed over decades. This sort of relaxation will be years in the making. It is not the sort of thing where you will see instant results, as The Clench will only unfold when it is clear that you can be gentle with yourself and others. Like a turtle hiding in its shell, The Clench will close up in the presence of harshness or mistreatment, be it from yourself or others. Our goal is to mindfully bring about a deeper relaxation within you.

Many mindfulness practices include body scans in which you mentally look for the places in your physical body where there is tension and then work to bring relaxation to those spots. The instruction might include intentionally clenching a muscle and then allowing it to relax. What I'm asking you to do is to mentally find more than just the physical parts of you where there is tension. You could look at where the tension exists in your mind, and within your emotions. Notice the tension in your thinking. See where your emotions are closed off and shut down. Then bring relaxation, gentleness, and loving-kindness there.

What I imagine happening when you relax The Clench is that you will find deeper peace. Love will take precedence over control and protection in your life. In a way you will become more youthful and more open, but at the same time more wise and mature.

My hope is that our interactions in session will be Clench reducing. Seeing that we can stay safely connected and sharing ourselves with one another in session might help the clenched parts of us find relaxation. A lot of our clenching came from previous hurtful or disappointing human interactions. My hope is that as we get to know each other even more, our work together might contribute to loosening and expanding that which was previously closed.

Fondly yours,
David

Dear Elizabeth: A Blanket of Shame

Dear Elizabeth,

I don't think that your shame is actually an emotion. It's not like grief, happiness, or frustration, which can be emoted. Just try to express your shame. There really is not a face or sound that comes with it. Shame is a sort of silent inner stagnation that, unlike sadness, anger, fear, or joy, can't necessarily be expressed and released.

I see shame as a blanket that covers your emotions. It weighs down what you are feeling and keeps you from authentically expressing what is going on inside. I can tell how heavily this blanket weighs on you, Elizabeth. The crippling effects of shame show up in our every meeting. Any time you start to express a frustration, longing, or even some sort of joy, you mute or qualify it. Despite thinking quite highly of you, I often feel I have to be extra careful not to say something that will be taken as shaming, thus shutting you down.

Shame has that shutting-down effect. Just like a heavy blanket, it keeps out the cold; but it also keeps everything else out. It is hard to get closer to you because of it, and it seems difficult for you to get out from under it to touch the world. That is how shame works. It flattens everything.

Even more paralyzing is what happens when something good gets in past the shame. It hurts. When love, care, tenderness, or even the most basic validation of someone seeing you gets in, there is resistance. Instead of love inspiring us, it feels threatening, because it hasn't been there for so long. Like sunlight reaching watery depths seldom seen, it blinds the life forms living there. Care feels suspicious when it touches the uncared-for parts of us hiding behind shame. Tenderness seems intrusive. Validation feels exposing. Even though we might long for love, care, tenderness, or connection, it hurts when it finally comes in because we are just not used to it.

Elizabeth, it often feels to me that you don't believe I am truly interested in hearing what is happening in your life. I know that you were half joking when you said the only way I could listen to you each week is that I am getting paid to do so. It couldn't be further from the truth for me! I really do care about what is going on with you. I actually am interested in your life. Yet the shame that riddles you keeps any care I might have from really making a difference. Feeling ashamed about who you are leads you to not believe me when I say that I can relate.

My goal is for you to get a sense that I truly do care, and that in letting one person in, such as me, your therapist, you might feel more comfortable letting others in. My hope is that in sharing with me more authentically who you are, you become more comfortable doing so with others. In a way, therapy is practice. It is sort of a relationship laboratory. If you are comfortable being seen by me, then you might be open to letting others see you as well.

First we need to figure out what to do with the blanket of shame that enfolds you. If you were hampered by another emotion such as fear, then we might consider finding a way for you to discharge the fear so that it is no longer within you. If your grief kept you withdrawn and detached, then we might find a safe way for you cry out some of that sadness. Yet with shame, there is no way to discharge it. As I said, I don't think of shame as an emotion that needs expressing; instead, shame needs to be unlearned. It needs to be shed so that you are more free to connect with the world.

To shed it you need to start recognizing it. Together we can look at how shame shows up. What are the defeating thoughts that are shame based? What is the body language you display that is associated with shame? What is the inner dialogue that tells you that you are no good? Becoming more self-aware, and recognizing when shame shows up, is the first step. Being wise to how shame governs your inner and outer reality can help you get out from under it.

Once you develop a practice of recognizing shame, then we can work on detaching from it. There is no need to resist it, for what you resist persists. Instead, we need to name it. Giving an emotion words allows us dominion over it. Saying within yourself, "Oh, I am feeling shame right now," allows you some distance from it. It allows you to master the shame so that it no longer controls you.

Once you are able to name the shame when it arises, you will have more freedom to replace old thoughts, feelings, and even body language with what suits you better. We might entertain thoughts and feelings that are more affirming to you. We might consider emphasizing the gifts that you have to give the world and accentuate those qualities. Once you recognize shame and name it, the choice becomes yours.

Shame is a straightjacket around your heart. It keeps you from being flexible, authentic, and free. It can often reach the core of your being and immobilize you from feeling love. At a deep level, you need to recondition who you know yourself to be. Instead of being ashamed of your longings, desires, idiosyncrasies, and secret joys, you could start sharing with me who you are. Therapy is a place to start practicing.

Fondly yours,
David

Dear Adam: Find Your Fuck It

Dear Adam,

Thank you for telling me about your experience at the triathlon last weekend. Knowing how obsessive your thinking can be, I realize it was quite an undertaking to have trained for the triathlon and completed it. When you told me that you became quite overwhelmed, anxious, and paranoid at the beginning of the running stage, I would have figured that you would have taken yourself out of the race; learning that your training team also left you behind, I would not have blamed you for pulling out. Yet the fact that you finished the race shows something very important about your character, which I want us to explore.

I asked you how bad the anxiety and paranoia was at the worst part, and you scaled it at a 10 out of 10. It was your worst panic attack ever. Yet there you were, at the finish line, looking back, having completed the race. When I asked what you did in order to get through the entire running portion, you told me that you said to yourself "fuck it" and kept going.

This fuck it moment was a breakthrough, in my opinion. When you could have become overwhelmed by emotion, something arose within you and took control. You found a way to keep going, despite every inkling to quit. Something within you was stronger than the obsessive thinking. You said "fuck it" and took control of your mind. I am very impressed.

My hope is that you can find again this internal control going forward. May you master your own mind so that it does not throw you to and fro. Instead, demonstrate the same determination and grit that you showed at the triathlon. In order to do so, I want us to take a closer look at what it meant for you to say "fuck it."

That moment did not call for positive inner talk. It did not call for trying to quiet your mind and take deep breaths. It called for stepping out of your thoughts and throwing all care to the wind. It called for something deeper within you to emerge and take control of the situation. Your fuck it moment was a birth of a stronger you that had more to accomplish that day than entertaining the myriad thoughts and feelings that usually distract you.

If you were driving across town to get to the grocery store, you would not stop in each house along the way to look in the window and try to understand what was happening with the people inside. Instead you would pass each house on your way to your destination, the grocery store, primarily undistracted. The same thing goes for our minds. We don't always have time to address each thought that comes our way. We can't always indulge in the feelings we have. Instead, we focus on the task at hand. Sometimes we might notice a thought or feeling here and there, just like we might regard a nice house or garden on the way to the store, but it doesn't stop us from focusing.

In the case of the triathlon, Adam, you had a goal. Even though the anxiety of being in a large crowd was very loud in your mind, and even though your obsessive thinking was at level 10, you found a way to focus on each step of the race toward the finish line. I am proposing that you find that same determined focus in your everyday life. Be up to something much bigger than your thoughts and feelings. Keep your eyes on the destination. At times your mind will be loud and hijack you, but that is where you can draw on your fuck it moment.

You can remember that something much more determined exists within you. Right now, we can call it your inner "fuck it," but over time, I think you will come to identify more with the grit and determination inside you. Instead of seeing the upsetting thoughts and feelings as who you are, you might anchor yourself in your strength of mind. We haven't seen that mental strength before. It has been dormant. Yet at one of the worst moments, that strength showed up to propel you. Let's not have to wait until you are under duress for this aspect of you to come online. Let's find your fuck it right now.

To do so, you might need to care a little less about your thoughts and feelings. You might need to release them rather than engage them. "Fuck it" suggests that you are not investing as much in mental planning, safety, or vigilance. It throws caution into the wind, and takes a more expansive and bold perspective. Fuck it breaks things, gets dirty, makes mistakes, and is messy. Fuck it is not aggressive, but busts the mundane barriers of ordinary life and helps you accomplish the extraordinary … like completing a triathlon.

Let's not stop there, Adam. I invite you to release some of the constraints that keep you occupied between your ears, which prevent you from connecting more deeply with others and feeling more involved in the world. I invite you to see that life exists between you and the world. It lies in the space between you and other people, not in the endless thoughts, feelings, and interpretations that run through your mind each day. Getting out of yourself and into the world might require more of those triathlon moments. To get more into life, you might have to simply say "fuck it."

Fondly yours,
David

Dear Rachel: Paralysis by Analysis

Dear Rachel,

There is a tremendous misunderstanding that permeates almost all of Psychology, which says that if we understand something, then we can heal from it. While diagnostics are important, many well-meaning clinicians get stuck in making sense of the problem without knowing how to actually resolve it. You are very much caught up in this misunderstanding and I want to make sure that we don't get stuck in it in our work together.

You know very well what has been causing you pain. We don't need to identify it any further. Instead of us diagnosing the problem, let us use discernment to find your truth. Making sense of what ails us only gets us so far, yet we move into real growth when we recognize that the problem in and of itself was probably not ours in the first place. It is like throwing out the garbage. You want to discern what is garbage and what should not be tossed. Yet once it is clear what is trash, then it gets thrown out. Psychology tends to rummage through the garbage in people's psyches to try to find answers. We cling to the psychic trash, using old and outworn thoughts and feelings to determine our personality.

Rachel, you are steadfastly attached to the notion that your life is unfair. Your experiences in life have shown that you have to do all the work—that if you don't take care of it, then nobody else will. Growing up as the second oldest child of seven, you were always tasked to take on more duties and chores than the rest of your siblings. In many ways it was unfair, but it was also the best way for your family to function as well as it did. You were indeed burdened, and you have continued to bear that burden in your family of creation, doing everything for everyone and feeling like you never get a break. You are, as you say, the last on the list when it comes to the family's priorities.

Like most of us, Rachel, you could spend decades analyzing what it means to be taken for granted. You might be encouraged to express your feelings in ways you couldn't have done growing up. Traditional psychotherapy focuses on meaning, action, and emotion. It helps people develop insight into their struggles and to take steps to resolve them. This is all very good, yet the therapy of today does not show people how to clear their issues and create something entirely new in their lives.

The difference between analyzing and clearing is that when you recognize, make sense of, and take steps to resolve your issues, you become embroiled in them. You identify with the problem and become attached to it. You resist the problem and it persists. You read more about the problem, tell your story, and then perpetuate it. Rachel, when you started working with me, you told me the story of cooking and washing the dishes for your family countless times, in various permutations. You were attached to this story that your life is unfair, and were thus suffering from paralysis via analysis.

Understanding our problems and trying to make sense of them is a very human approach. It is normal to attack the issue this way. You are not alone in this tendency. Yet, like the rest of us, you end up stuck right back in the same problem because you don't clear the issue entirely from your life and open up new space for something new. To clear the issue, you need to discern who you truly are from who you have come to know yourself to be in relation to the problem.

Consider for a moment that this issue of life not being fair is not even yours in the first place. Perhaps your deepest truth is that life is wonderful, abundant, and easy. As a child, you may have been more inclined to see life as a fun adventure in which things come and go, and to believe that things always seem to work out somehow. This may have been closer to your truth before you started having experiences in which you learned the opposite. I am not saying you didn't have painful experiences of injustice and loss. I know you suffered as your needs became ignored and you were tasked with caring for your siblings. What I am saying, however, is that the interpretation of life being unfair, and identifying yourself as someone who always comes out on the short end of the stick, is a paradigm from which you need to completely unplug. "I'm the bottom person on the totem pole" needs to be a story that gets tossed in the trash as the old, outworn debris of a developing self that it is.

You have known yourself to be a person who takes on the extra work and doesn't see the payoff in the end. Your identity and personality have been shaped around this real and lived story. The adventure of true therapy begins when you start to de-identify from the thoughts and feelings associated with this story. When you claim that this pattern of relating and behaving is not yours in the first place, you start to see dramatic changes in your life rather than a series of little incremental, yet often easily reversible, steps.

Please see that your distress is not yours in the first place. The story that life is not fair is not yours. It has been around for a while and graced many a bumper sticker, impacting many people's psyches. It's a collective picture in which many of us live. The hook is that you personalize this picture, make the story your own, and then run with it. You carry the suffering as a badge of honor, yet no matter how much you and I analyze the symptoms, and problem solve the latest iteration of the dilemma, you still stay as the protagonist of this story of suffering. I invite you to step out of it altogether. I implore you to clear the thoughts, feelings, sensations, and behaviors associated with this canard. The words you use in your conversations, and more important, the words you say in your thoughts to yourself that convey a sense of your old story, need to be discarded like yesterday's news because that is what they are. They tell a story you already know. They are nothing new, and if I join you in these old stories then I don't serve you in ways that bring out the best in who you are.

Instead of us traveling down the old roads of analysis, let us focus on clearing. We have to discern what is you from that which is something you picked up along the way that no longer serves you. You will know your truth: because it will feel good to you. Lies never feel good. Maybe the story that hard work pays off feels good to you. If so, then that may be your deeper truth. If the narrative that life is not fair feels pretty awful to you, as I imagine it would, then perhaps it is not your truth. It is an old lie that needs to be crumpled up in a ball and tossed into the wastepaper basket of old stories of who you thought yourself to be. Once clear, my sincere belief is that the true you will emerge.

Fondly yours,
David

PART VI
Conscious Masculinity

A SHIFT IS ON. There is a new form of masculinity arising in today's modern men. It is a change from old ways of being to emergent new ways of existing. It is about undoing old patterns of boyishness, sacrifice, or sexual acting out and stepping into new realities of personal responsibility and reliability.

Today's man has the potential to be both masculine and conscious, to be someone who is direct and firm, but also gentle and wise. He is sensitive and potent, successful and loving. He faces both joy and sorrow, virtue and vice, with a strong heart and a clear mind. He recognizes the ingrained patterns in his life and engages to take on the automatic internal responses that have gotten him and his brothers into trouble throughout history.

Today's man has been let down. He has become disillusioned by religion, schools, families, and the prevailing image of a man as purely functional, without feeling, needing to have it all together. He moves into adulthood, realizing he is ill-prepared to take on the challenges ahead of him. As a result, he roams the world in search of meaning, yet is often left focusing only on the basic tasks of managing and avoiding painful experiences. He tries his best to put on a positive veneer and find courage. He becomes the "company man" or the "good solider" in an attempt to get ahead and feel alive. Yet, sadly, over time, he realizes that this is not bringing him what he wants.

Men have not been given a clear framework that tells them how to be a man. They may see models of masculinity and what men do in the world, but often only an external representation and a set of rules, not a guiding set of principles of how to handle life's vicissitudes and circumstance. Today's men have not been given paths for personal growth and transformation that will take them out of the archaic, brutal ways that have existed throughout time. Historically, he has not yet seen how to fully take responsibility for his own life. Yet today's men have a chance to grow. As they do, their families and those around them benefit.

The following letters are to men who are on the forefront of their own personal growth. They are struggling with core issues that most men face. I see them as some of the pioneers who are helping craft a new model of conscious masculinity. My work with them is a privilege and I hope it opens up new possibilities for other men.

Dear Brian: Man as Lover

Dear Brian,

Sensitive men promise the sun, moon, and stars. They take us to places we have only dreamt of. They lift us to heights and open new possibilities within our souls. Sensitive men hold the promise but they rarely deliver.

Where is the sensitive man when things get messy? Where is he when the grotty, icky stuff of life gets in the way? Usually he is bailing out. He flees to his dreams and leaves others to do the heavy lifting. He finds a way to put it back on others rather than doing the hard, emotional work himself.

Brian, my man, it's clear that you are a magical guy. It's no surprise that women gravitate to you. You know how to be charming and playful, and make others feel special. Even when you say hello to me at the beginning of our sessions, I feel liked by you, and it feels good. It's your charm, but charm has gotten you into trouble.

Anytime your relationships have gotten too real, you've bailed. You've left when the going got tough and then found other outlets. Instead of creating deep and lasting love with your wife, you've sought endless excitement and pleasure with numerous women. It's a shame, because had you really invested in your marriage, it sounds like it could have worked quite well.

Instead, you had a tentative touch. You were flighty in your marriage rather than bold. And now that you find yourself divorced, with a new relationship, it pains me to see that you are repeating this tentativeness. Instead of being bold in love, you are fleeting. I get it. I know how hard it can be to hold down real intimacy with another person. Yet it also upsets me to see countless men playing loose and free with love.

Rather than honing and grounding the power of masculine love, the sensitive man plays a boys' game of love 'em and leave 'em. Yet,

Brian, you are capable of so much more. If you wisely wielded the power of your masculine energy of you as Lover, then you could bring so much good into the lives of those around you. You have a gift, but you need to learn how to use it!

Our work together is to put internal structures to your loving. We are finding ways for you to have discipline with your love: how to channel it effectively, and how to stay present even when you feel overwhelmed. Rather than running away, pretending, deflecting, blaming, retreating into your shell, shrugging it off, playing aloof, or lashing out, you are learning to create clarity in your relationships. You are learning to set the tone you want in your life and articulate clearly what you are thinking and feeling. It is deep and far-reaching work that can have great impact.

Your work is to go deeper into yourself. Your charm has been your escape from building depth. The world needs more men who can go deeper and harness the gift of their masculine love. Families benefit from a father who can honor his word and focus his love. Communities thrive when men deal with the hard stuff and deliver on their promises.

The boy inside the man will always be there. You can still be sensitive and charming and magical. Those qualities need not go away. They can, however, be filtered through a more adult version of you, one that sustains presence and can remain when things are tough emotionally. Think of the way you handled disagreements in your past marriage. They were seen as an annoyance. You did everything you could to avoid sitting and talking with your ex. When eventually she convinced you to talk about the relationship, you would belittle her and minimize her concerns. It was a set of elaborate avoidance behaviors intended to keep things light, and to make her feel silly for saying anything to you. You would try to cheer her up and take her out rather than together getting to the bottom of your issues.

Yet now it has been encouraging to see you start to change your ways in your new relationship. Even though initially you started utilizing the same avoidance behaviors with your new partner, you began to see that if you kept doing what you were doing, you were going to keep getting what you have gotten. Now you have found a willingness to stay and talk. You are less concerned about winning an argument than you are about understanding her and being understood. These are good steps toward important changes. I see this growth in you as something that can extend well beyond you. This is about you showing others what a conscious and present man can look like.

I imagine that if you can make this change, it might touch hundreds of people. I imagine what sort of impact you might have in the world. It excites me that we might be able to make that much of an impact with our work together. That is why I push you so hard. That is why I challenge you when you do the same old sensitive man-child thing. I see what is possible for you and for those around you. You are a great guy. Now go be an amazing man.

Fondly yours,
David

Dear Thomas: Man as Killer

Dear Thomas,

I have been thinking a lot about the story you told me last session. With a heavy heart I keep replaying the scene you described on your recent trip to Europe with your wife. It has stayed with me for days, partly because of how much I care about you, but also because I think it touches a deep nerve. Your story exemplifies what a lot of men are struggling with today.

To hear that you and your wife were stuck in an airport for a six-hour layover at first just sounded to me like an inconvenience. Yet to hear how you watched when another man began to chat and flirt with her in the airport lounge, that was wince inducing. When he had his arm around her and you reported that you just sat paralyzed, not doing anything, that made me quite upset and angry.

I can see how you might sit passively and not want to cause a scene. I understand how confused you might have been in that moment. Were you supposed to go over there and threaten him? Were you supposed to pull your wife away from the scene and scold her? Were you supposed to be the "cool guy" and sit by to let this continue? I think I speak for most men when I say that I feel for you. It is confusing in this day and age to know how to be tough.

What was illuminating for me is that after you let this go on for over an hour, your wife became quite upset with you. She was frustrated that you did not come over and do something about this. She wished you had at least checked in on her. Sadly, she has become accustomed to you doing nothing; but this enactment brought each of you face to face with a painful dynamic that exists in your marriage.

You have dialed down your masculinity to dangerously low levels. While trying to be caring, sensitive, and egalitarian, you have neutered yourself to the point that it causes painful scenes like this one in the airport. Your passivity has left your wife feeling deeply alone, having to fend for herself. In your efforts to be kind, you have become a wuss.

Someone needs to confront you about this. You know I care about you, so it might as well be me. Yet know that you are not alone, Thomas. Many modern men have done the same thing. We have all seen how problematic toxic masculinity has been throughout the ages. Men have been warring, pillaging, and plundering for centuries. We have caused most of the world's problems. Being a man has been synonymous with causing pain. If the choice for us is either to be a man and cause pain, or to not be a man and care for those we love, most of us choose the latter. We have become less masculine as a way of not repeating the injustices and atrocities of men of the past. We have chosen not to end up alienated and alone as a result of our regressed and bone-headed actions.

The problem is that we have thrown out the baby with the bathwater. We have discarded a core aspect of masculinity in our attempt to be more enlightened. We have forgotten how to be a killer. A fundamental aspect of masculinity is to protect. If there is a saber-toothed tiger outside the cave, we do something to protect the family. If there is a threat, we eliminate it. Be it a spider, financial stress, car troubles, or a stranger's arm around our wife, our job is to destroy that which is causing danger. Yet we have lost our destructive nature as a result of seeing previous men killing wantonly.

I know that your father was a pretty rough guy. You have told me about how he often got drunk and threatened your mother. When he was angry, it sounds like he was a scary dude, throwing things, yelling, and abusing his power. You told me how you vowed never to be like him, and you have succeeded. As a father and a husband, you are nothing like him. You are kind, sensitive, attentive, and caring. You don't drink and you don't threaten anyone. Yet in this process of rejecting your father's archaic ways, you have ended up being the softie who sits paralyzed in the airport lounge, failing to defend your marriage.

Thomas, we need to develop your killer instincts. It is vital for you to foster your ability to kill off anything that threatens what is sacred to you. There is no risk that you will turn into your father, but you need to reclaim some of his "piss and vinegar" so that you can stand your ground when needed. My hunch is that your wife will appreciate you developing a stronger backbone. She will enjoy your conscious power.

Many men with whom I work are in a similar position. Their issues are not that they are abusive, angry, or acting out; rather, they are struggling with powerlessness, ineffectiveness, and acting in. They are more depressed than angry. They have dialed down their masculine energy to a point to where they are easily pushed around. I share this with you to let you know that you are not alone in the confusion. We are all trying to figure it out.

The confusion comes partly from the fact that the threats today are not as external as they used to be. There is no saber-toothed tiger outside the cave. Instead the danger comes from within the family. It comes from the interpersonal disagreements, or the emotional cutoffs that occur in relationships. The arena of the family is the modern proving ground for men. Less so is it about the battlefield, the sports arena, or the business world where a man's mettle is tested. Instead it is in our close relationships that a man displays his worth.

It is acceptable in business for us to count our net worth, or "make a killing," yet in family life we are still trying to figure out how to best have an edge, speak our truth, bring our presence, and love with all our might. Your task, Thomas, is to imagine how you would have ideally eliminated the threat to your marriage in that airport lounge in Europe. We can turn that painful episode into a gift. Let us keep envisioning the man you would need to be who would swiftly remove the danger without it causing any further problems. You won't cause a scene like your father might have, nor will you sit passively any longer. Let's imagine you as lover, as killer, doing what needs to be done.

Fondly yours,
David

Dear Michael: Sexual Confusion

Dear Michael,

I want you to know that I hear how alone you feel. I understand how much you long for your ex-girlfriend. I hear your struggles with trying to hold back old patterns of using dating and sexual encounters to avoid your feelings.

Loneliness is very painful. I think it has many layers. It is not just solely about companionship with another human being. It is not just about sex or about someone being there to validate your existence. I think that loneliness can be a symptom of being soulful.

You describe a sort of loneliness that I think comes with you being a solitary man. It is a pain that is deeper than the fact that nobody is sitting next to you at a particular moment. It is an existential longing for feeling deeply a part of something bigger than yourself. It is an emptiness that nothing worldly can fill. Yet you exist in this world. You have to find a way to live day to day while carrying this emptiness, knowing that no consumption, no relationship, no experience will truly fill it, for it sounds to me like a spiritual void.

I don't think sex cures this sort of existential loneliness. A deep connection with nature, the Divine, plants, animals, food, music, poetry, etc., seems to come close to filling this void, yet perhaps nothing worldly can. Perhaps you can find connection with the pure little things in life. Perhaps you can look to soft moments, brief encounters with ordinary magic in the world. Maybe those little things can fill you rather than sex. Yet ultimately, like the rest of us, you will have to find a way to manage your confusion around sex.

You have been describing to me a struggle over whether or not you should have sex with the various partners who are available to you. You have been trying to hold back, and not use sex as a salve for your weariness and loneliness. I say have sex if you want. Enjoy it! Just don't think it has anything to do with loneliness. Healing your loneliness is a separate endeavor altogether. Have sex for sex's sake. Then nurse your loneliness elsewhere.

Please know that there is so much confusion for all of us about sex. It feels good. We come from sex. One could say that life energy is sexual energy. Yet just like life, sex can be lived in many different ways. It can be given away, taken, devalued, and repressed. Also like life, sex can be celebrated, cherished, enjoyed, and treated as sacred. You might consider that your misuse of sex is akin to your devaluation and degradation of yourself. The ways in which you use sex for personal gain is equal to how critical and harsh you are with yourself.

I try to project lovingkindness and compassion to you in each meeting. I do this so that you might take it with you, so that perhaps you will start to treat yourself more gently. You push and pull on yourself. You treat yourself as if you are some sort of science experiment, analyzing and dissecting everything you do. Your critical voice is loud, and I wonder how much you then turn to sex to try to bring relief from internal criticism.

It sounds like you long for sweetness and healing in your life. You are currently dating a nice woman named Beth who works at your local coffee shop. Even though you do not find her as exciting as your ex, Katie, whose exciting corporate job takes her all over the world, Beth is honest and cares about you. You have been trying to build a relationship with Beth, but it is interesting to see how the more you are ambivalent about her, the more you try to fill the gaps with porn and flirty texts to other women. The more you starve yourself of connection with her, the more you reach for something unhealthy.

My hope is that you could instead reach out for Beth and find solace in the real connection you have with one another. Even if she is not your soulmate, you have still created a good structure with her in which you can ground some of your longing for connection. Perhaps you can find a way to enjoy the human connection that is there rather than chasing the ones that no longer exist.

I know it does not necessarily feel this way, but what you have with Beth is healthy. What you had with Katie was not. Yes, it was exciting with Katie, but ranch-flavored potato chips are also exciting. They just aren't healthy. Your relationship taste buds are still accustomed to the taste of junk food. Beth's kale chips are boring to you, even if they are healthy.

You tell me that you are scared to let go of the flirting and romantic practices that you have used to try to fill the spiritual lack you feel. Please know that these are two different things. Spiritual lack has nothing to do with sexual, flirty romantic practices. Go have flirty interactions with Beth. Enjoy them. Just know that they will not do anything to fill the spiritual lack. Flirting is flirting. Enjoy it if you want and don't feel guilty.

Yet for your spiritual lack, what is different now is that you have so many more tools than you have had before. Now you can draw on your ability to connect with the little things in life to deal with the lack. In fact the spiritual connection can be easy. The sexual one is what is confusing.

I hope that some of this helps with the questions you have about sex and loneliness. I have faith that you will find your answers.

Fondly yours,
David

Dear Wayne: Your Great Undoing

Dear Wayne,

I usually don't take any voyeuristic pleasure from hearing the details of how clients live their lives. Even though people will sit down with me and start opening up about the full range of their experiences, I take being on the inside of their lives as a privilege, not entertainment. From behaviors they are ashamed of, to unexpected triumphs, to romantic drama, it runs the full spectrum, and I am with them in it.

However, I have to say that with you, Wayne, I can't help but get caught up in the drama of your life. It is difficult not to be captivated by the life you lead. The level to which you have risen in your tech business is stratospheric, and the range of travel and experience that comes with the company you are building is quite impressive. I don't feel that I live through you, but my interest is piqued on a regular basis about what will happen next in your world.

It doesn't feel like you are trying to entertain me in session. I think that you know I would be here, caring about you, even if you were living an everyday, run-of-the-mill life. You are an affable person who shows up for people. Your brilliance and passion is admirable. The business that you are building is a reflection of who you are, not what defines you. Yet with all that you have going on, the range of high-level business dealings, the international travel, your wife and young child, your emerging reputation and notoriety in your field, all of it can be undone by one thing: your attraction to other women.

I know that you love your wife, and care about your family. I know that you are trying to make sense of who you are, and remedy problematic behaviors. When you recant story after story of flirtations with other women—how they come on to you, how easy it would be to bed them, how there are a few you just innocently chat with on the side—I can't help but become very worried. I know you are not bragging when you talk about these dalliances, but that you are honestly wrestling with how to manage your sexuality so that it doesn't undo everything that you have created and value.

If we know one thing, it is that in this day and age, a man's misuse of sexual energy can completely undo him. We do not have to look far into the headlines to see great men humiliated by scandalous behavior; men who have good reputations, emerging power, and everything to lose, throw it away on sexual affairs, dirty pictures, and sexting. You, my friend, are headed down that same road. I have seen it over and over with countless men who let their attraction to other women ruin everything they have.

It starts innocently enough, and they chalk it up to guys being guys; but far too many married men end up interested in, flirting with, talking to, dating, sleeping with, or engaged in a relationship with another woman. You can be assured that you are not alone in this behavior. Men struggle with how to channel their sexual energy into a monogamous relationship. They have a sort of sexual dragon inside of them that they cannot tame, which gets the best of them in dramatic and highly consequential fashions.

All of this is meant as a warning. It is not like you have nothing to lose, and I would be remiss to sit back and watch you continue down this road. It is a balance for me. I deeply believe that you have your own answers. I am not here to give you my answers, for they don't even always work for me! Instead I am here to help you be in touch with your own native wisdom, and help bring out the best of what is possible in you. I have made great mistakes when I have tried to get clients to live their lives differently. Who am I to say what they should or should not do? We all are learning from our experiences, and who am I to stand in the way of that? Yet when the learning experiences are excruciatingly painful, I try to see what is reasonably possible for me to do to help the client avoid some of the excessive pain of losing it all.

What causes the most problems for men in your situation, Wayne, is their deception. The duplicity often demonstrated in the pursuit of satisfying sexual urges erodes the trust of those around them. When spouses, investors, or customers learn of these devious ways, they assume that these men are a fraud through and through. It is impossible to get that pure trust back, so I ask you to be open to finding a new way.

Part of the trouble for some men is that they need to have or possess the object of their desire. It is not enough for them to see someone who they find attractive, or even talk with her briefly. No, they need to flirt, to know that they could "have" her, to get her number as some sort of proof of their virility. They may need to go so far as to actually consummate their sexual fantasies. Might it be possible for you, Wayne, to just feel enlivened by an attractive woman? Could you feel how her presence energizes you, instead of needing to "move in for the kill," as you said last week? Could you then bring that enlivenment home to your spouse rather than spread it around all over town?

That is, unless you would prefer to be a bachelor. This would be a construct that would allow you, in this day and age, to meet, flirt with, and date as many people as you wanted. The structure would be set up for you to have multiple flings if you need to. There would be no deception because you declare yourself a bachelor. There is a lot of loneliness with this sort of life, but you would be free to get your "ya yas" out. Bachelorhood may not be a realistic choice for you because I know that you love your wife and child. It would be a great loss, but you can't have it both ways.

If you choose to stay married, you will need to develop discipline with your sexuality. You will need to harness it and channel it in ways that match the type of man that you project yourself to be. The word discipline gets a bad rap in the Western world. It is usually associated with punishment. However, I think you might find clarity and strength with knowing that you can develop mastery of your sexual energy. Others might even respond to you in new ways, feeling your new-found control and focus. Your marriage might experience a renaissance if you consistently bring home your playful, lively, lusty energy.

It can be difficult to grow in this way, and we will figure out how to make these changes if you are up for it. Just know that you are certainly not alone in this struggle. Many modern men are trying to figure out how to be more conscious with love and sexuality. We are moving into a new paradigm of what it means to be a man in this modern era. A lot of it has to do with this core issue of love and sex. You are right there, on the front of the wave, evolving.

Fondly yours,
David

PART VII
Finding Love

THE SEARCH FOR LOVE is one of the main reasons that people come to therapy. They are either painfully single, struggling in an unhealthy relationship, or suffering from a break up. The aches and pains of the heart are often too much to bear alone, and people look toward counseling to help them get out of pain, or to at least help make sense of the confusion of love. Love makes a fool of us, and brings out our best, as well as our worst, qualities. We run headlong into romantic relationships, only to have them chew us up and spit us out.

I think that the reason so many people come to therapy to talk about relationships is that we are all learning about them. There is so much that we don't know about mate selection and finding love in this modern era. Only recently in the course of recorded human history has choosing a mate been based upon love. The criteria we use for finding a partner has changed so much in recent times that people are very confused about how to find, sustain, and enjoy a healthy romantic relationship.

We are all learning how to have healthy relationships. Nobody has it figured out, so I don't see any shame in people seeking support when it has to do with matters of the heart. We are either foolish, powerless, painfully alone, or bound up in attachments. We want so much from our partners, yet often struggle with the definition of appropriate boundaries. People compromise themselves in order to make relationships work; they lose who they are, become dependently attached, and often long for what they used to have.

These letters are to dear, brave souls who are playing full out in the game of love. They put themselves out there to find real, meaningful connection. Yet, like most of us, they encounter difficulty and confusion. They wrestle with loss and longing, and enjoy joy and exaltation. I see relationships as the fast track to better knowing ourselves. Relationships are our greatest mirror and reveal much of who we are. By looking at how we show up in closest connections, we can find a lot of information about what makes us tick, while also learning how to be ever more effective in the game of love.

Dear Tanya: Be a Fool in Love

Dear Tanya,

We should talk about love. We ask so much of our partners in today's relationships. Our unions used to be about political arrangements, dowries, or procreating so that we had more hands to help on the farm. Nowadays we are looking for our partners to be our lovers, friends, companions, co-parents, and co-CEOs of the family. Never before have we asked for so much from our romantic partners. New paradigms of what a relationship can look like are emerging, while at the same time we have so much to learn about love itself.

Romance and love bring out the best and worst in us. Matters of the heart can be as exhilarating are they are confusing. We get hurt over and over, only to return, seeking more love. It is as if we can't help but run headfirst into love, even if it means costing us our well-being.

As the thirteenth-century Persian poet and Sufi mystic Rumi put it, "I would love to kiss you. The price of kissing is your life. Now my loving is running toward my life shouting, what a bargain, let's buy it."[5]

We know that love may cost us dearly, but nonetheless we run toward it shouting, "What a bargain!" Perhaps this tells us something about the value of love itself. We will do anything for it. Yet it also shows us how foolish we can be with our hearts.

This foolishness seems unavoidable. I hear from countless people like you who make poor choices in relationships. There is a reason that Shakespeare said more than four hundred years ago that love is blind. He, like Rumi, knew of the divine fool that love makes of us all. People are really good at letting us down in love, but even in the face of this disappointment we run headlong back into the drama of romance. I encourage you, Tanya, not to beat yourself up for making these same mistakes in love; instead, embrace the divine fool within you.

In the Tarot, the Fool is considered both the first and the last card in the Major Arcana. It is the fool who gets us on the path of the great mysteries of life. Without the fool, we would not start out on the journey of love. Our naïveté gets us into trouble but it also opens up new possibilities. To embrace our inner fool might make us more forgiving about the errors we make in the game of love because everyone has a divine fool within them. Knowing and working with our own fool might allow us to proceed with more wisdom.

The main mistake that most of us make in love is the one that you shared with me last week. You described how lost you have become in the powerful connection with your new partner. You described a euphoric sense of being in love, yet the fear of becoming completely engulfed by it is terrifying. You recounted a level of ecstasy like the ones written about in songs and described in fairy tales. I would never want to disillusion you of this feeling, but I think we should be clear about where this love emanates, lest you lose yourself any further.

The love you feel in this relationship is like the moonlight. It is enchanting and mysterious, and it leads you to want to bathe in its glow. Yet its light is not its own. It is reflecting the light of the sun. Be clear that the love you feel from your partner is merely a reflection of the love within you. Your lover does not generate the euphoric feeling. You do. Romantic love makes it feels like the other person is bringing us joy. However, it is helpful to recognize that the love we experience is just a casting back of our own loving heart.

Fools in love sing of the stars shining just for the two of them. They wonder why birds suddenly appear every time their love is near. Yet those stars are always shining, and those birds are always there, too. It is just the experience of being in love with another person that connects us to a higher level of awareness. I share this perspective with you not to encourage you to give up on this relationship, but instead to proceed with wisdom. There is no need to cling to your partner as if they are the sole source of love in your life. They are not the sun, but merely the moon in your sky.

For if you can step into your own connection to love itself, Tanya, then you might be able to sustain intimacy in this relationship. The fool within us tends to lose ourselves in the other person. When two become one, we experience a profound, almost spiritual, connection. Yet if we become enmeshed with the other person, any ground for sustained intimacy deteriorates. We need differentiation. Knowing that you are over here and the other person is over there allows for a healthy separation. It allows for a relationship.

Similar to Georges Seurat's Pointillist paintings, in which small dots of color are applied in patterns to form an image, when you are up close to the work all you can see are the dots. You get lost if you are too close. Yet, as you get a bit of distance, you start to see the bigger picture. You are able to relate when you have some space. Instead of losing yourself in the relationship, it might help to have some psychic space. Find a sense of the "me" that can stand on its own amidst the gravitational pull of the "we" of the relationship.

For if you have a sense of yourself, then you may more fully experience the mysteries that come with love, and especially sex. Most of us get lost when it comes to sex. It's one of the most misunderstood aspects of human relations. We come from sex. Life energy is the same as sexual energy. It's the very core to who we are, and gets misused all the time. Perhaps even worse, people allow sex to be routine and predictable. They close off to the mysteries of sex, just as they become numb to the mysteries of life. They shut down and become defensive. Instead of loving one another, couples start to fight with each other. Too much fighting leads them to abandon one other.

Rather than getting caught up in the typical fight-or-flight response that dooms many relationships, I encourage you to stay and love. This fight or flight tends to override even the most loving of individuals. Instead of collapsing in fear, I encourage you to stay open to love.

I realize, Tanya, that I am asking a lot of you. I am asking you to embrace your foolishness when it comes to love, to own your sense of self so that you don't become too enmeshed, and to stay open to the mysteries of love and sex while not getting caught up in typical fight-or-flight responses. It is a tall order when it comes to modern love, but I think you are up for it!

Fondly yours,
David

Dear Joanne: Become Fiercely Loving

Dear Joanne,

I don't completely get it. How did you make it that many years in a marriage that was so one sided? How did you go for so long with such mistreatment and neglect? I guess that is what we are working on together: to better understand how your marriage became so imbalanced.

What you report to me are endless stories of your loving and giving nature, and how what you received back for twenty years was dishonest, inconsiderate, and lackluster treatment. I know that there are two sides to every story, and that you have been quite honest about how you let the marriage slip away, yet there is no denying that you have a good heart and a caring soul.

So how does someone like you end up in such an unhealthy relationship? Many of us ask that same question. It is a rampant occurrence that good, highly evolved people create relationships with people who mistreat them. It is as if these old souls are taking on projects of less-developed individuals. It is like you are a karmic love missionary out to rescue the weary and downtrodden. Why are there so many of you who are more enlightened but accept crummy relationships with less-than-stellar partners?

It has been an honor to witness you stop this pattern and recover from your divorce. You had already done a lot of the heavy lifting before you came for therapy with me. You had drawn your line in the sand, left the marriage, and taken a stand for your worth and well-being. I am not surprised that you've come as far as you have post-separation, yet I still don't completely get how the strong woman that I see in front of me today put up with such schlock in her marriage.

Perhaps we can dissect that for a moment, as I know that you are not alone in wanting to understand how your relationship transpired the way it did. Most of us don't go into relationships seeing the pitfalls and imbalances that await us. We usually feel swept up in a connection and, if the timing is right, we build a life with that person. Yet it seems that over time, the true nature of each partner emerges and we live in an arrangement that we didn't quite see coming. Some pull the ripcord and leave when they see the real person in front of them. Others just accept what they unconsciously signed up for and make the best of it. Still others try everything they can to make it work despite compromising themselves. They jump through hoops, adjust their expectations, work within new parameters, stretch themselves to cover the shortcomings of their partner, regularly rise to the occasion when the other does not, and if need be, find a way to live with years and years of second rate, inadequate love. This third group sustains themselves on the metaphoric junk food of malnourishing love. They are not sustained by their spouse's love, but find a way to stomach it anyhow.

You, Joanne, seem to fall into the third category, which maybe is not as pathetic as I make it sound. You tried everything you could to make it work. You learned how to live with B-level love for twenty years. You rose to the occasion time after time, stood in your integrity, and did what was right for your family. You didn't sit passively by, but instead tried to bring out the best in your ex.

You tried, and we can't fault you for that, but our work now is to better understand how you went so long with such mistreatment and neglect in your most primary relationship. We might consider that this was an imbalance between love and power within you. You were a loving spouse—on that you can rest assured—yet the question is how can modern women and men be both loving and powerful?

What if you had been more fiercely loving in your marriage? What if you had been uncompromising, relentless, insistent, and demanding, while still being completely warm and open hearted? I think that this would be new territory for most of us, as there has been a gross misunderstanding in our Western world about what it means to be loving. We have been taught that meekness, patience, and kindness is loving. We have confused being nice with being loving. We have been conditioned to turn the other cheek and let bygones be bygones. We thought that it was divine to go with the flow and not rock the boat.

In the Eastern world, however, they add another sort of loving: that of fierceness. Buddhism and Hinduism include fierce deities who are depicted as scary and even demonic-looking. They are known to be the most loving friends, as they protect that which is sacred. Perhaps we could take a page from their playbook and learn how to be ferociously loving, not compromising of our boundaries, and stand powerfully for what is sacred.

You have taken great stands throughout this divorce. You have demanded fairness and have learned how to navigate complicated emotional waters with poise and efficacy. In doing so, you have sent a deep, loving message to yourself that you are worthwhile. Though you have known your worth all along, this new firm stance has been a fierce embodiment of the love you deserve.

Your newfound power will not scare the right people off. Instead they will feel your clarity. Your communication will ring with authenticity, and your love will flow freely in balance with others who regularly acknowledge your worth. This is great work you are doing. I know that countless others will learn from seeing this example you have set. I already have.

Fondly yours,
David

Dear Jared: The Power of Attachment

Dear Jared,

Sometimes I think that attachment is more powerful than love. As humans we are wired for attachment. In our most intimate relationships we form a bond which helps us feel securely attached. When this bond is ripped out, it hurts like hell. In fact, when people come to my office to talk with me about breakups, they sound like they are in hell. They tell ongoing, countless stories about the nuances of the demise of their relationship.

"First he texted me (this), then I replied (that), then he didn't write anything back for twenty minutes, but I could see that he read the text. Here, let me read you what he wrote back."

I let them read the text, and go through the gory details of how it all fell apart. They search for clues of how they might have stopped their world from coming undone. It is maddening for them. I say to them, as kindly (and as wryly) as possible, "You are temporarily insane."

I know that this is not what they are expecting to hear, and I am not trying to be mean. I am actually trying to reassure them that their state of mind is crippled by the pain of an attachment bond being ripped out, and that the pain will eventually end. Every loss like this builds on itself, like a bruise on a broken bone. The current breakup hurts but also hits a deeper wound of earlier losses. When this wound explodes inside a person, it is like they are transported back in time. Old emotions flood in, and they lose any sense of being able to think clearly.

The emotional centers in their brain fire off. They have what we could call an amygdala attack. The amygdala is the older emotional center toward the base of the brain. When it fires, we lose access to our prefrontal cortex, which governs reasoning, language, and problem solving. The prefrontal cortex is the more developed part of our brain. So when these deep attachment wounds flare up, and an amygdala attack takes over, we quite literally lose our rational mind!

I don't mean to lecture you on brain functioning here; rather, I want you to honor that you have a keen ability to attach. You are able to bond with others on a deep level. It is a wonderful thing, but it also leaves you vulnerable when that bond is severed. You have already loved, and lost, and loved again. You have attached and detached and reattached many times. You have been like emotional Velcro, bonding, un-bonding, and then re-bonding again. This is healthy!

Though you have been through this over and over, it doesn't seem to get any easier when you lose someone you love. I know how much you miss your ex. I don't want to take that away from you, nor could I. You can hold on as long as you like. I am not here to tell you to let go and move on. I just ask you to look at your choices here.

You say you want to move on. Yet you talk a lot about the times you spent together with your ex. Over and over you recall the details of the time you met through friends at a trivia night, of how you used to both love horror films, and following the news together. You recall the weekend getaways and how you learned to cook with one another, yet then you talk about how so many things didn't work and how difficult it was when you fought. You spent so much time thinking about how you would like to create something new.

From where I sit, it looks like you have two choices. You can hold onto your ex, or you can go about creating new possibilities. I just don't see how you can do both at the same time. If you are grasping onto the old, then your metaphorical hand is closed, and it can't reach for something new. If you let go, then your hand is conceivably open to grab hold of what is next. One choice might not be any better than the other. Perhaps you want to stay holding onto what was. That's completely fine, and I am with you in that. Yet please do not think that you will be creating something new when you are holding onto the past.

When you are ready to open to your future, I will be there with you as well. Maybe we will have to bury the past ties that bound you. Maybe we will have to sever any last remaining thread that links you to your past. Yet, one thing I know is that when you are ready, you will indeed love again.

Be patient. Be gentle with your heart. It has great capacity for love. It moves at a rate different from your mind. It takes its time, and has a wisdom all its own. It attaches, it feels pain, and it loves.

Fondly yours,
David

Dear Sarah: Faith Is a Thing

Dear Sarah,

I hear you when you express your longing for love. It is almost as if there is a deep aching, a moaning from your soul, that yearns for reunion with your other half. You have tentatively talked with me about soulmates and twin flames, worrying that I might judge that sort of perspective and offer you a more practical mindset instead.

Yet it doesn't really matter to me whether soulmates are actually real, or if they are just a psychological construct. That sort of argument misses the point of your deep desire for something you do not have in your life. It is remarkable to me how much you already have: your career, your personal growth, the solid love from your family of origin. Yet your desire for a spouse and to create a family makes it feel to you as if you have nothing.

I am not here to tell you that in order to find love, you have to work on yourself, love yourself more, or focus on something else; or that when you aren't looking, love will find you. Instead I want to tell you to keep faith. Believe that you will find love. You see, faith is a thing. It is a complicated phenomenon that together we could examine more closely.

Faith is not binary. It is not like you either have it or you don't. Faith exists on a spectrum. You might believe that you will meet your match in the next year, yet your level of faith may wax and wane from day to day. You might become doubtful, like after the painful experience you had a few weekends ago when you were out solo with all couples. At those moments of intense not-having, your doubt creeps in.

"Why is it not happening?" "What do I need to do in order to be in a loving relationship?" "How long will it take?" "I should just give up." These are normal thoughts. I can't tell you how many people long deeply for a healthy romantic relationship. I don't believe it's because we are pumped full of images about love from cartoons or romantic comedies. I believe we long for love because somewhere inside of us we know it is real. We know in our hearts what is possible.

When life sends us challenges, and when things don't go how we planned, then it is easy to lose faith. We forget the deep inner knowing because our outer reality doesn't reflect what we know is possible. We project the current outer reality into the future and become fearful that the lack we know today will continue. It is important for you to watch this process within your mind, to see how you go from belief, to hope, to painful experience, to doubt, to hopelessness. Just track how you get off course. Watch how the old stories of feeling "something is wrong here" keep replaying themselves.

When you believe that something is "wrong" with you, or with your life, then all you see are problems. All you see is what you don't have. Yet faith is the opposite of "something is wrong here." Faith is willfully believing that something is right. It doesn't mean you have faith that things will work out. Faith is unreasonable. You believe because it feels better to believe than not to.

Try this: Live as if you already have the thing you are longing for. In this case, live as if you are in that loving relationship. Be the person you would be if you were in love. Generate those qualities yourself rather than relying on outer conditions to dictate your well-being. Notice how this is different from longing. When you are longing for love, then you are longing. There is nothing wrong with longing. Some say that longing for love is indeed part of experiencing love itself. Yet if you are tired of longing, then switch to having. Having is what faith looks like. Have the treasure of abundant love, which is in you already, and it will be easier to have faith that the relationship you wish is right around the corner.

Sarah, I know that this is not an easy process. The suffering of the heart is real. Sometimes it is not easy to be single. Yet while we can see that faith includes a sense of "havingness," faith is also about power. When you have faith that it will happen, then you are standing in your power. When you doubt that it will work out, then you are in a place of powerlessness. Faith equals having, and faith equals power. Doubting and longing are about "something is wrong here" and about powerlessness.

I want you to understand that it is utterly human to feel like something has gone terribly wrong in your life and to feel powerless. These are aspects of the human experience. You will have plenty of moments when you feel doubtful, vulnerable, and ineffective. Yet when those moments happen, perhaps you can switch to identifying them mindfully and, with compassion, gently shift out of those states of being. You can indeed choose to enjoy what you already have in your life. You can indeed choose to be powerful. Enjoying what you have, and powerfully believing that your life is working: that is what faith looks like. I encourage you to believe.

Fondly yours,
David

PART VIII

Loving Each Other

COUPLES COUNSELING IS TRULY exhilarating. Being with two people as they work out the stuck places in their relationship takes attention, stamina, and deep care. People's most core and primitive issues are on display in couples counseling. They act out their personal and relational dramas in the room. It is an honor, as the therapist, to be on the inside of their relationship and help them find new possibilities.

Working with a couple is really like working with three clients. There is each person, but there is also the relationship. Their relationship is my client, and my job is to help it exist and thrive. My goal is to get the relationship to be the healthiest it can be. Often this comes in the form of teaching new strategies and relational tools, as most of us do not have a lot of experience in relationships. We simply do what we have seen our parents do. We get stuck by approaching the relationship in a prescribed, routine way. We don't often bring our creativity. We usually repeat the same patterns, and hope for something different. We focus on our partner and find ways they can change, rather than taking up new ways we can show up.

Learning to love more effectively comes not just from learning new tools but from practicing them in the session. Couples counseling differs from traditional therapy in that it is more alive and active in the session. There are more enactments of the clients' issues in the room. Rather than the couple talking about how they might be more expressive of their love, I invite them to start expressing it there in the session. I might ask one person to turn to the other and tell them how they are feeling. These enactments bring the work to life, and often raise the intensity. Couples who are willing to take on this sort of work often find that it changes the ways in which they relate.

Rather than being stuck in old patterns, they find new ways to connect. Today's couples are often quite disconnected. They are stressed and overwhelmed with working, caring for children, and trying to run their daily lives. Couples report feeling hopeless, uninspired, and in a rut. Worse yet, they start to be unkind, uncaring, and unreal with one another. My work is to help them get back to being kind, loving, and authentic. The goal is to help them be creative in their loving, and not give up on what they have. Most people think that they have done everything they can to save a failing relationship, but usually they don't try even half of what is possible. My goal is to get them to see new ways of making things work.

These letters are to couples with whom I have been doing deep and sustained work. They come regularly to session to work on their relationships. Though they have a lot going on in their lives, they have made their relationship a priority. I find that very inspiring, and do my best to get them to a better place. My hope in sharing these letters is that they might connect with other couples going through something similar, and help them find new hope.

Dear Alex and Jamie: Who Does the Dishes?

Dear Alex and Jamie,

Our last session was the third time in the last two months that you have argued about who does the dishes at home. The latest episode was one in which Alex left a cereal bowl in the sink in the morning before heading off to work. Jamie, you reported seeing the bowl but did not wash it, even though you had some time to do so. Instead you waited to see if Alex was going to wash the bowl after coming home. That didn't happen, so you let it sit there in the sink until the next morning to see if Alex would say anything. He didn't, and that lead to an argument.

The cereal bowl in the sink was a symbol. It held tremendous meaning for you, Jamie. It was not just something that holds breakfast cereal; it became a test of who picks up after whom. The bowl became everything that is out of balance in this relationship and how you might take one another for granted. I can't tell you how many times I've heard people in therapy discuss who does the dishes. It is a very common conversation, as it represents something foundational in family life. The home is where we come together to share meals. Buying food, cooking, setting the table, clearing it, and washing the dishes are all daily chores that go into a shared family life. Yet the division of household labor constantly gets well-meaning and loving couples into ongoing quarrels.

Doing dishes is the grunt work of mealtime. We speak about the joy of cooking, we watch cooking shows on television, and take great pride in preparing a healthy and hearty meal for our families. We also go to great lengths to savor food. We become foodies, try new restaurants, and revel in good company over a shared meal. Yet we do not celebrate the joy of doing dishes. There is no dishwashing competition on television. We don't see shows about adventurous hosts traveling the world in search of people doing dishes. No, the dishes are reserved as a chore. They take a back seat to the main event of the meal.

Those who are left to tend to the dishes might also feel like they take a back seat. Being charged with the grunt work of cleaning up after dinner might feel lower status than being the one preparing the food, and it certainly feels lower than those who are being served. The dishwasher can feel taken for granted and unappreciated, almost acting in a service capacity.

Jamie, when you saw Alex's bowl in the sink, perhaps you felt that he was sending a message that you should wash it for him. Perhaps you felt taken for granted and in a service role. If that's the case, then I can see how that would feel awful. The next day your argument escalated over this cereal bowl. Alex, you felt Jamie was being ridiculous to get so upset about a bowl. In fact, you felt pretty hurt yourself that Jamie would wait to see if you would eventually wash the bowl and test you in this way. I know that this isn't the type of environment in which you want to live. The argument stretched on for days and turned into extended periods of silence until you came to our couples counseling appointment.

Of course you know that this was not about the cereal bowl. The level of emotion and argumentativeness far surpassed the indiscretion of leaving a bowl in the sink for a day. We need to understand what was brewing underneath the surface such that it boiled over during the cereal bowl incident. We need to look at why people get so upset about who does the dishes.

You are not alone in this scenario. Who does the dishes represents so much about the structure and dynamics of a family. Why do some people share the task of dishwashing while others split the tasks and relegate it to the person who did not cook? In your relationship, Alex and Jamie, how is the division of household labor handled? We need to examine if you are holding any deeper resentments. I would suspect, Jamie, that you are carrying resentments about certain aspects of the relationship, and that they came pouring out when you saw Alex leave his bowl in the sink.

Often what will become illuminated for couples is that issues are buried deeper than they realize. There can be a displacement of relational emotions onto household duties. Jamie, you have talked before about not feeling like a priority to Alex. You've described him as someone who tends to be more concerned about his own needs, and who neglects yours at various times. It is no wonder that in the aftermath of the cereal bowl incident, you brought up that he was not around for you when your mother was sick in the hospital. Alex had no idea why you would bring that up, and became quite defensive. Yet if we look at it together, we can see that the deeper tides of neglect and lack of appreciation overflowed when the bowl was left in the sink.

The bowl wasn't causal; it was merely illuminating imbalances already existing in the relationship. It brought to the surface the problems in the marriage that you have not yet addressed. Brave couples, such as you, are willing to look at times when a fight over the dishes turns into something bigger. They are open to investigating what the fight is telling them about their relationship. This cereal bowl incident can be an opportunity for greater insight and connection. It can be a chance to better understand and care for each other. Once you start feeling one another's enduring care, and once you feel less neglected, then you might see the cereal bowl differently. It might just be a bowl. It would not carry the same meaning that it did the other day. When that felt sense of care is present, you might not worry about who does the dishes. Instead you might actually volunteer to do them!

Fondly yours,
David

Dear Maria and Bill: Get Real

Dear Maria and Bill,

It is difficult to work with you. I am frustrated because I value being close to my clients in our work. If anything, I can rely on moments here and there in session when there is great honesty, and we look at an issue together. Yet in our couples counseling together, I find those moments few and far between. I find myself far away from you, and try as I might, I don't yet know how to get closer.

However, you sit so close together on the couch. You hold hands often. There is excessive canoodling. I don't mind honest displays of affection, but yours feels like a defense of sorts. It is as if you snuggle with one another as a way of not having to look at the difficult issues in your marriage. I worry that you are pretending to be close when in actuality you are both so far apart, lonely, and in your own worlds. I worry that you need the marriage to be okay so that it can hold up your lives; that if we expose the problems, they would crush the image in your minds of what the relationship needs to be. It is with true kindness and compassion that I ask you, I implore you, to please:

Get real!

I know that marriage counseling is difficult. Just the notion of us meeting means that we have to look at what is actually going on. Being in the room together, we know it is a space where the veils of perception fall away. Our task is to better understand what is real. My sense is that this task brings up great anxiety for you. When you look on your calendar and see that tonight is couples counseling, you say to yourself, "Oh no. Not today." Yet I bet that what's under the dread or irritation is an anxiety about getting real with one another.

I can deal with that. I can be with people who are ambivalent about the work. Yet you would have to be real about being ambivalent. You would have to be honest that this work is bothersome. We can pace it so that it is not too uncomfortable. You would have to admit that you have been doing everything in your power to avoid the work, including deflecting, zoning out, not saying much of anything, dissociating, changing topic, using humor to avoid, and shutting down altogether.

I have learned the hard way not to push past people's entrenched defenses. When I have tried to hold people's feet to the fire, they get really upset. So I have been quite gentle with you both, not doing much that you don't want to do. I try to foster the small embers of work into flames that might warm your marriage. We had some great conversations about your ski trip in Canada and how you felt young again. We looked at ways of bringing the early days of the relationship into present time. Those were great sessions, but then our work fell back into usual conversations about the daily stresses of running your home-based business together and how tired you each feel.

I worry that I have become less real with you myself. I have colluded with you to be a bit false. It doesn't feel good to pretend with you, but I have not known what else to say or do. I don't even know what we are avoiding. I guess I have been avoiding directly expressing the frustration that is coming through in this letter; but beyond that, I don't know what we are tiptoeing around. What is so difficult for us look at?

I wonder if it is frustration and anger with one another. I have no basis for this other than that those emotions are part of what I am feeling. When I have become disconnected and unreal with myself and others, it was because I was infuriated. I wonder if you are so angry and enraged with one another that you have no choice but to be lovey-dovey, lest your anger come flaming out and burn your marriage.

Forgive me here that I am taking a stab in the dark, but are you angry at how disappointing the other person has been? Are you enraged that the other has let you down? Do you resent a double standard? Are you tired of having to cater to one another's neurotic needs? Has sex become a formality? I don't even want to ask you these questions for fear that I will not get a real answer. I worry that you will deny any bad feeling. Even if you do admit to feeling disappointed or angry, I am afraid that we will only touch on it in a cursory fashion.

Yet I am not one to shy away from a complex puzzle. How do I get you to buy into the fact that getting angry at one another can save your marriage? It's a tough sell. It goes against all of our instincts. We run from conflicts. Yet in the early stages of our work together you acknowledged that you seldom argue, and never really fight. You agreed that this could be a part of the problem. However, we got away from that. We got lost in other topics, as we are wont to do.

Instead we should come back to how going through conflict can bring you to real harmony. We should look at how if you were angry at one another, that it would be okay, and that you might feel even closer by authentically working through your differences. If you break through into your anger, you might find deeper love. Then when you snuggle, it will have all the feelings of a couple who has really been through the wringer; a couple who has faced down their shadows, who have walked through the unbearable with one another and come through the other side, fire tested, with the battle scars to prove it. When a couple like that canoodles, it warms the hearts of those around them.

I want this for you, and you will have to forgive me if my tone here has been harsh. I'm not used to feeling this way about clients, but maybe I have had to fight with you in some way. I have had to get real with you in order for the couples' work to go deeper. Maybe something good will come from me expressing my frustration, just like it might in your marriage.

I am frustrated, yes, but still quite fond of you. Writing this letter has made me realize that those two feelings can indeed coexist. So I mean it when I say ....

Fondly yours,
David

Dear Annette and Richard,

I thought it was interesting today when we stopped the conversation mid-sentence to talk about how flat things felt. You were reviewing an argument you had last weekend when, instead of plowing ahead as usual, we looked at how it felt in the office in that moment. I know that you both felt cut off, but it was remarkable how you each revealed that you were not very interested in the conversation about the fight. You knew where it was going, and could predict exactly what the other person was going to say, yet were willing to plow along anyway.

It almost felt robotic the way that you were hashing out the events. We were just putting the train on the tracks and redoing the same conversation you have every time you fight. There is usually a lot of point/counterpoint, he said/she said, heady back and forth about who was right. We don't really cover any new ground when we do that. Yet today, something made us stop and look at what the heck we were doing. None of us were really that engrossed in the discussion, but we all felt like there really was no other option other than to get through it.

It was a microcosm of your relationship. You have become so familiar with one another that a lot of your relationship, like our conversation today, is predictable. I call it the comfy sweatpants syndrome. You become so comfortable with one another that you do the same routine over and over and enjoy it. "Good old comfy sweatpants over there. He's exactly how I expected he would be!"

Being comfy is not all bad. We want our partners to be familiar. We pull for familiarity so that we can safely attach to them. Familiarity is good. It has the same root word as "family" for a reason. We like predictability, so we turn our relationship into a pattern of familiar dance steps, so easy to follow that we could do it in our sleep … and unfortunately we often do become asleep in our relationships.

Yet just as much as we want comfort and predictability, we also crave new experiences. We want to keep things fresh. We want excitement and sexual novelty. Familiarity is the enemy of eroticism. It keeps us from experiencing one another in new ways.

Richard, could you consider that Annette is a complete mystery to you? Though a part of your mind (your ego) wants her to be knowable and familiar, she is a mystery to you and unto herself. Annette, could you consider that even though you can predict exactly what Richard will say and do, that he is an enigma you will never fully understand? Though a part of you likes him to be comfy sweatpants guy, another part wants to experience him through new eyes each day.

If this sounds even remotely possible to each of you, I invite you to become more creative in your relationship. Please don't keep doing the same things over and over and expect different results. It has been said that this is the definition of insanity. Let's try to change things up in how you interact with one another. Most couples report that they do the same thing over and over in the bedroom. Their sexual routine is predictable; it seldom changes. It becomes a well-worn rut.

All of this routine is a failure of imagination. Like many couples you don't think outside the box. You don't try anything new. You have a set range of reactions and responses to one another. You keep going to the same well time and again, and then you wonder why things are not changing. Perhaps instead of doing the same, we could try creating new routines. We could discover new ways of interacting which you have not yet tried.

Couples counseling is about discovering these new ways. It involves changing up the conversation so that alternate possibilities arise. In sessions, I add a new voice, interrupting the regular rhythm of how you talk to one another. I throw curve balls in there to disrupt the call-and-response patterns of your interactions.

I know it is frustrating for you, Richard, when I cut you off in the middle of you explaining how a particular situation went. I know that you want to get your perspective out there. Yet Annette's body language each time you go into these long explanations conveys at best disinterest, and at worst mild disgust. It is more important to me, as your couple's counselor, to address and interrupt this counterproductive interaction. Neither of you benefits from Richard going on and Annette tuning out. When I cut you off, Richard, we should look together to find a way to do something new. You each could approach the interaction differently.

I will keep interrupting the old when we meet, if you will fill in the space with something different. The question is, what would you want that would be different? What do you imagine would add new life to your interactions? I look forward to seeing what you create.

Fondly yours,
David

Dear Priya and Sam: Be Kind to One Another

Dear Priya and Sam,

A family can be a dangerous place to grow up. While it is where we find our sense of belonging and connection, where we discover who we are and learn about the world, it can also be rife with harmful and toxic interactions. The high levels of disrespect and micro-aggressions that often occur in families cause all sorts of troubles. They shape our belief in ourselves, our level of generosity, our behavior in future relationships, and our outlook on life. I believe that families are the cornerstone of our society. If we make them safer and healthier, then our world will be a better place. All of this is a way of me saying to you today: Be kind to one another.

It is exciting to see you embarking on a life together. The dreams you have for starting a family are lovely, and I wish you all good things in your marriage. I also wish you a lifetime of being deeply kind to one another. Too often marriages fall into a place of relational violence. Domestic abuse is more prevalent than we might think, with anger and force dominating the landscape. There is no place for any sort of abuse in relationships, especially physical. It destroys families.

Emotional abuse is just as toxic. It has a corrosive effect on relationships. Couples often speak to one another with a level of disrespect and derision that they reserve specifically for one another. Belittling, minimizing, and shaming, we cut down the ones we love rather than build them up.

When I first meet with a couple for counseling, I notice the tone with which they speak to each other. Just as important as what they are saying is how they are saying it. Are they cutting one another off or finishing each other's sentences? Are they invalidating and belittling or are they respectfully disagreeing? Does their body language convey disgust and contempt or are they open and connected? Often couples don't even realize to what degree they are being disrespectful or kind. How they speak to one another is in their blind spot.

When the moment is right, I will let them know what I observe. I might say, "Even though you're in a tough place in your relationship, the way that you're speaking to one another today is very kind and gentle. I think this gives us a good chance of remedying the situation." They like hearing that, of course. Some couples have even high-fived each other when told how lovely their relationship is!

What they don't like hearing, and what I wait to say until they feel safe enough with me, is that I observe a level of interpersonal violence in how they communicate. "I'm noticing how Bob always cuts off Susan when she's speaking. Do you guys notice that?" I will try starting with something reflective like that to see how they respond. It is not easy to look at interpersonal emotional violence, but like the proverbial elephant in the room, we need to address it.

We have talked about this in session, but I want to express it here, how troubling it is for me to see the gas-lighting going on in your marriage. Gas-lighting is when one person interacts in a manner that makes the other feel that their perceptions are invalid; that they are making things up. The term comes from the 1938 play *Gas Light* in which a husband makes his wife think she is going insane by refuting everything she says. I don't know if you fully see it, Sam, but you have a way of telling Priya, every time she expresses something with which you disagree, that she is wrong. This causes her to shut down, and worse, question whether or not her perceptions are actually valid.

This level of interpersonal violence needs to stop, as it may very well undo all the good things you are creating in your marriage. I invite you to consider a more postmodern approach to your relationship. One in which both of you can have different views of reality, and that they can both be valid, even if they are different. Can we let go of a notion of Truth, with a capital T, and consider that you each have different but equal experiences of a situation? We spend too much time in session going over the detail of an event. There is a lot of he said, she said going on. It is often difficult to get to a resolution, because you are each trying to convince the other that your perception of what happened is the right one, and that the other person is wrong. I wonder sometimes if you are more interested in making the other person feel crazy than helping them feel loved.

It is really a choice, and the choice to make the other person feel crazy feels like a violent one to me. Our world is crazy-making enough. We don't need our intimate relationships to make us feel any smaller than we already do. Yet, like many couples, you regress into cutting one another down with your words or withholding your love to spite your partner. You play one of the worst games of all when it comes to love: that of take away. You pull away your love from the other person when they do something that hurts you. It is petty and threatens everything you are trying to create.

What can I do to help you be more kind to one another? Be clear that I am not a referee and won't be declaring one of you the winner at the end of each session. Your relationship is my client. I want what is best for your marriage. If I could give you any wedding gift, it would be that of a lifetime of lovingkindness toward one another. I wish it was something I could just give to you, because I think it would help hold up this union for a lifetime. Instead, kindness toward one another needs to be practiced and cultivated. You need to make a habit of it. You need to curb your reflexive need to debate, criticize, defend, or devalue, and replace it with a practice of slowing down, listening, staying open, and supporting one another.

This would be putting your love into practice. Others will feel it when they are around you; they will recognize that this is a couple who honors and cherishes one another; that they treat one another gently and with compassion. Most important of all, your future children will be able to feel it and will be raised in a family that is truly safe, that honors their perceptions, and encourages self-expression. Who knows what would be possible for those children if they grow up in a home such as this? Who knows what would be possible for our world if all children did?

Fondly yours,
David

Dear Donna and Steve,

I don't think there are any easy answers for how to navigate our parents aging. You each shared in great detail what it is like to be in the "sandwich generation." You have to care for your growing children and your aging parents at the same time. The implicit expectation is that you should have the strength and stamina to respond to everyone's needs.

And there is some reality to this expectation. Your children should not be expected to fend for themselves. Yes, there is a lot they can do now that they were not able to do before. They can help make their own lunches, and they don't have to be constantly reminded that it's bedtime, yet when it comes down to it, they are in your care. You are the ones who contain them. You are supposed to be stronger.

The same goes for your parents. There is a point where the onus is on you, the adult child, to care for them. It's up to you to call, to ask them how *they* are doing, rather than expect that they primarily care for you. It may not be clear when this moment comes with your parents, but at some point it changes. You are the one in charge. While this might be helpful in some ways, it also puts you in the role of caretaker for both your parents and your children.

This has led to you both feeling depleted, as if there is not enough time, care, love, or attention to go around. It all gets gobbled up by your children and your parents. Maybe you have occasionally a few moments for social media or to catch up on a television show together; yet I hear both of you report that you want more from your partner, even though you feel you have nothing to offer of yourself. Though there is so much good in your life, it feels like a deprivation state when it comes to care and affection.

While we would normally suggest taking time for you individually and as a couple, I think that a paradoxical approach is called for here. Rather than do less, I suggest you deepen your commitment to being caregivers. Yes, it would help for you to carve out date night, or have an evening at a hotel away from the kids; but on a day-to-day basis, I encourage you to deal more deeply with your parents aging and see more clearly the burgeoning development of your children. By recommitting to being caregivers, you might experience your daily demands with a renewed attitude.

Let's look at your parents first. It can be terrifying to see them age. A part of us wants our parents to stay strong and active, like they were when we were younger. As they become more frail, we realize that we are stronger than them—not just physically, but emotionally, mentally, and relationally. Being stronger than our parents means that we are not kids any longer. We are fully adults. Our youth is no longer front and center. In fact, it is our children who get to be kids. We are fully adults, and that doesn't always feel so good.

By letting Mom and Dad age, you are letting yourself age. Though a part of you might not want to let go of your parents, at some point we are forced to realize that we will end up in this world without them. At some level you both realize that when that happens, even more emphasis will be placed on your relationship. You will have to lean on one another more. It will be important for us to talk about what that might feel like. My suspicion is that your concerns about this get expressed in indirect ways. Your fear about whether or not the other person will be steady enough to hold you up gets turned into testing one another to see if the other can really handle it.

Steve, I think about the time that the two of you came back from the hospital after visiting Donna's father. Almost immediately when you got to the parking lot, you began to fight with one another about the kids' schedule for the next day and who had the responsibility to drive carpool. This seemed like classic displacement about your feelings about Donna's father's ill health. You fought rather than wept. You bickered rather than talked about how scared you were.

I say that this is classic because couples do this all the time. Our emotions come spilling out sideways. Though we may not mean to, we take out our frustrations on one another. We lash out when we really feel vulnerable and overwhelmed. We try our best not to project it onto the kids, so it ends up going to our spouse. Your relationship has built up scar tissue from years of this. As a result, it does not move and flow as it used to.

This is partly why I suggest that you deal more directly with the aging of your parents. Put the attention onto what it is like for you to face this eventual loss. Go into the grief, fear, or anger. Instead of running from your feelings, lean into them. Have the conversations that you need to have with your parents. Many people wish for one more day with their parents so that they can say the one thing they didn't get to say. Do what you can, what is actually possible, to get to a place of closure.

With your children, I invite you to revisit your desire to have a family. Remember why you signed up for this. Try regularly to feel more deeply into your love for them. I know it is not easy when they are being demanding, but perhaps a practice in which you regularly feel your love for your children would be beneficial. When they are not around, for no reason, feel into the love in your heart for them. This sort of gratitude practice may allow for you to be more expansive and creative in your parenting. Share with one another how you feel about your children. Express to each other the many things you appreciate about your kids. You'll be surprised how much that makes you love one another more.

All of this is meant to try to change your perspective while being in the sandwich generation. Some of your circumstances we can't change; but the way in which you experience it, we can.

Fondly yours,
David

Dear Joan and Larry,

I am sure you have heard the story about the person who falls into a hole and stays there, struggling around in the dark to get out, until they finally find a ladder to climb out. The next day they are walking down the same street and fall into the same hole. Yet this time instead of struggling around in the dark, they know the ladder is there, and they climb out more quickly. The following day they are walking down the same street and instead of falling into the same hole, they walk around it. The next day they take a different street.

This is a story of learning from experience. All of us fall into a hole at some point, and all of us struggle to find the way out. Yet over time we learn to avoid the pitfalls that beset our path. We grow, and can anticipate when something unpleasant might happen. We make necessary adjustments to avoid more unpleasantries in our lives; yet in relationships, most of us keep falling into the same hole, and keep struggling to find our way out. For some reason, learning in our most intimate relationships is more difficult. It takes a lot more time and repetition. Perhaps this is because we are blinded by our pride. We are more concerned about looking good and being right than about learning to love more effectively. We are more easily threatened in our relationships because it can bring out the worst in us.

In our last session you described a series of exchanges that have been occurring, in one form or another, over many years in your relationship. You had a disagreement if your teenage daughter should be allowed to stay out later at her friend's house. You had differences of opinions, and a quick, charged exchange ensued in front of your daughter. Instead of taking time to talk about it, Larry, you said something sarcastic and cutting about Joan and her overprotective parenting. To this, Joan, you reacted in a dismissive way that marginalized Larry.

While your exchanges haven't always been specifically about parenting, the sarcastic and marginalizing tone has been pretty consistent. I know that you love one another, but your nasty tone invalidates one another. It belies the love that you have. You wonder why the intimacy has been diminished, but have been unwilling to see how these exchanges are like a slow water torture wearing away your bond.

Larry, would it make a difference to know that the word sarcasm comes from the Latin *sarcasmos*, which means "to tear flesh"? Do you see the sarcasm as something playful, or do you recognize the cutting and destructive impact? I see your use of sarcasm as an act of forcefulness in response to feeling disempowered. I can see how Joan marginalizes you, and how powerless you feel. I know that it feels like your opinion doesn't matter in this family, and that no matter what you do, you will be discounted. So instead of finding a powerful way to intervene and maybe change how things are handled in the family, you have resorted to force. You have become passive aggressive and say things to undermine your wife. This causes her to feel vulnerable as well, and to employ her defense mechanism of dismissing and minimizing you.

It is a cycle. You are bringing out the worst in one another because you feel threatened in some way. Your vulnerability has led to forcefulness. This has then caused you to take a cutting and sarcastic tone with one another. It has turned your marriage and family into more of a battleground on the subtle emotional and psychological levels. Outwardly, things look nice, but these toxic exchanges have started to poison the inside of your marriage. It is no wonder you have distanced yourselves from one another in order to stay away from these hurtful interactions. This distance has led to a lack of affection; now, a few years away from being empty nesters, you are looking at a future together that might be quite unpleasant.

To your credit, you have sought out counseling to take a closer look at what has been happening. You both would like to fix the marriage but don't know how. You keep walking down the same relational street and falling into the same hole, and you wonder why things look so dark. The question is if you are willing to really look at how you show up in the marriage and take steps to change it.

Instead of using force to cover up your vulnerability, are you willing to be more open? Could you drop some of your more subtly aggressive ways of engaging, and instead employ a more open and honest approach? It might feel more vulnerable at first, but it will be a more powerful way of engaging.

There is a difference between force and power. Force, psychologically and relationally speaking, is the use of more primitive means to manipulate or influence another. I see it as our last resort when we feel overwhelmed or don't know what to do. It is like when you are trying to parent a young child and you want her to come along with you to leave the playground. You try all the conversation and discussion possible before you resort to force. You pick up the child and carry her with you away from the playground while she screams and cries. This is a show of force. In adult relationships, force shows up by withholding love and affection, threatening to leave, talking or yelling over one another, bullying, lying, or becoming physically aggressive. While we might understand that force is a response to feeling powerless, there is really no room for it in a loving relationship.

Instead we want to employ a more powerful approach to our relationships. Power is the use of skillful means to create optimal possibility for outcomes that are in the highest good for everyone involved. Moment to moment, being powerful in a relationship requires assessing the situation and choosing what is most needed. Perhaps sometimes the right thing to do is to stop and listen to your partner. At others, it might be better to take a timeout and leave the room. With your heart in the right place, you will know what to do, but you have to be willing to pay attention to when you feel threatened and try to use your words to create a sense of connection.

Choosing power over force allows you to get back to what you believe in. It allows you to put into practice the love you have for one another. Right now your actions show that you are more interested in protecting yourself and controlling the other person. This is clearly a forceful reaction rather than a powerful choice of love. As we work together and slow things down, my belief is that we can step into a reality in which your love shines both inside and out. This may take some work, but I know we can get there together.

Fondly yours,
David

Dear Emma and Mark,

We have been working together in couples counseling for well over a year. With your busy lives, and your children's schedules, it is a testament to your willingness to work on your marriage that you have come in almost weekly. We knew from the beginning that there were not going to be any quick fixes. You are both very smart people, and if this was easy to fix, you would have figured this out already.

This has been a process of uncovering what is keeping you stuck in a marriage that feels loveless. What you are experiencing as a married professional couple with children is what many similar couples experience. I see this all the time in my practice. It is quite normal to put your relationship on the back burner when the demands of children and careers overwhelm you.

We have started to see things turn around for your marriage. Like a train moving in one direction, it takes time to get it to slow down and stop before turning it around in the other direction. We have had to slow down old patterns of behavior and the notion that you are driving your relationship full speed toward divorce. I know that it has been painful to look at how you have been contributing to the downfall of your marriage, but remember it took us months for you to shift out of simply blaming the other person for everything they do wrong!

It took time to slow down the unhealthy patterns and behaviors that have led us in this direction. We can look at turning things around and start building momentum in a positive direction, but I want to know that you are willing to really try. It's like a sports team that can feel proud that they put in their full effort. They leave it all on the field. Even if they lose, they can still take pride in that they did the best they could. I used to coach competitive basketball, and I encouraged my players to give me everything they had when they took the court. We wouldn't win every game, but it felt good when we put everything out there.

Are you willing to leave it all on the field with your marriage? Are you willing to try everything to make it work? This is not just for each of you, but also for the sake of your family. Most couples think that they have tried everything to make it work; but if truth be told, we would see that they haven't really even done half of what is possible. If you know in your hearts that you have done everything in your power to try to make this love last, then it will not be as painful if you do indeed need to divorce.

You wonder why things are bad and that you don't feel close? Well, you have not been investing in the relationship. The bank account of love is nearly empty and you wonder why! I ask you, what can you do to make deposits? What can you do to start investing in this relationship? The focus here is on what *you* can do, not on what the other person needs to do. If you take responsibility for your end of things, even in the face of the other person not doing anything, then you may start to feel more hope. At the very least, you may start to feel more power that you can impact the relationship positively.

Perhaps you could simply start to speak more positively to one another. Could you start to flood the relationship with positive expression? There are a lot of ways to express affection, and I am wondering if you would be willing to try again. We want to create a cushion of positivity on which your marital issues lie. If we build up a bit more positively expressed affection and fondness, then your issues won't hurt as much, and it will be easier for you to deal with them. A lot of couples feel hopeless that things can change. I want you to know that people can and do change, that anything is possible in a relationship. I have seen people come back from the brink of divorce to fall in love again.

Are you leaving it all on the field? Are you trying everything to make this work? Could you work with me so that you are? There is so much love here in this relationship. It just needs to come out. I want you to know that with courage, and a willingness to fall in love again, anything is possible.

Fondly yours,
David

PART IX

Finding Perspective

REFRAMING THE SITUATION so that it looks different is a lot of what therapists do. We help people see their lives in a new light so that they might discover new ways of approaching the situation. A reframe is a way of expressing an idea differently. In other words, we help people find new perspective in how they look at themselves.

My hope is to at least shift the way that my clients think about their problems. If we can find a new way of understanding how the issue arose, then perhaps we can find new ways out of it. What keeps a lot of us stuck is that we stay in a particular viewpoint and have a difficult time shifting out of it. We try everything we can within that mindset, but end up frustrated because we don't make a second order change.

A second order change is one in which we create a completely new way of seeing things. According to family therapy pioneers Paul Watzlawick, John Weakland, and Richard Fisch, second order change is the change of change. Whereas a first order change is one in which we make changes but the structure of the system does not alter, a second order change transforms the system itself. It includes changes in the rules that run the structure or internal workings of the system. In other words, it requires a new learning. It is what some have called a game changer.

When someone has this level of shift in their perspective, they see the world differently. They undo misunderstandings that have often built on themselves and caused even more confusion. Our work is to help untangle the mess of misconceptions and false impressions that people carry.

Helping people find a new outlook can take many forms. They might have a misunderstanding about the changes occurring in their lives, thinking they are regressing, when in fact they are growing. There can be accompanying confusion about what next steps they should take in their career, or perhaps there is resentment about having to be responsible all the time. However it presents, my goal is to help clients see things differently, and learn how to discern truth from fiction.

The following letters are ones in which clients are urged to find new perspectives. They have entrenched ways of thinking, and it takes a bit of disrupting their old ways to get them to make a second order change. Just as with Emma and Mark, if it was as easy as just suggesting that they look at things differently, then they would have already made a change. Instead it takes building trust, confronting misunderstandings head on, and being creative, through story or metaphor, to open up a new way to look at the situation. Once that happens, I believe that their innate wisdom will take over.

Dear Carlos: Catharsis Is Not Regression

Dear Carlos,

You are not regressing. I know it feels like things are falling apart. In some ways they are, but not in the way that you might imagine.

Yes, you are indeed going through something difficult. I get it that all the old ways that you have known are no longer working. You feel less effective at work, you have lost your mojo in relationships, and your sense of belonging is gone. What used to bring you pleasure is no longer interesting. I get it that it feels like something has gone terribly wrong and that what you are experiencing is a major problem. Yet I offer you an alternate perspective.

Could you consider that this is what personal growth and transformation looks like? This is catharsis. You are being stripped away of who you once were so that you might step into a greater version of yourself. It is like upgrading to Carlos 2.0. The old operating system (who you were before) was great. It was working just fine. Yet for some reason you are being called to upgrade into the next iteration of who you might be.

I don't exactly know why this happens for people. It is mysterious to me why and when people are called to upgrade. I know it when I see it happening; I can tell the symptoms from a mile away when someone is going through this sort of painful growth process.

The symptoms are a deep sense that your world is falling apart, accompanied by a sense that you are losing it. There is confusion, depression, a sense of everything moving away from you. There is loneliness, a new sort of emptiness that nothing can fill, and an existential sense of purposelessness. Sometimes people report physical symptoms of lightheadedness, inability to sleep, or aching in their legs. It is as if they are being uprooted, and in many ways they are. When I see these symptoms, I know that there is great growth occurring within that person.

Where the suffering intensifies is when the person clings to their old ways. Carlos, I see this in you on a regular basis. You wish to go back to how things were. You long for the old ways and how you were. The bad news is that we can't put the genie back into the bottle. You have already set off upon this path of personal growth; and as I said, I don't know why this is happening now, but I can assure you that it is indeed happening.

My speculation is that this process was initiated deep within you, long before you started feeling any changes. My sense is that even though you were immersed in your life as it was, there was some deeper part of you that was easily bored. It knew there was more to life, more to you. It saw what was possible, how you were subtly out of alignment, and it jumped up to the next rung on the personal growth ladder. It jumped and then your life fell apart.

What I am saying is that you chose this disruption to your life. You caused all of this to fall apart because you were going after more. On some level you wanted more of who you are, more of what is possible in life, and less of the subtle imbalances and ineffectiveness that were part of your old life. You can get angry with me for saying that you chose this, because why would you ever choose something that causes you pain? Yet if you see what you are going through as a catharsis, as part of a death and rebirth process, then you might find grace. You might be able to let go of the old and step into the new you.

I know it feels like things are moving backwards. You feel like you are regressing. Regression is when we truly revert back to old ways. It is as if we unlearn what we learned along the way and start making the same old mistakes again. Regression is backsliding, and you, Carlos, are not regressing. What you are going through is a catharsis. You are purging yourself of everything old that no longer serves you. Catharsis can feel a lot like regression because you are feeling all the old coming up again. You feel like you are backsliding, but the difference is that you are releasing those old, outworn ways once and for all. You can tell it is a catharsis because those old ways do not feel good anymore. They are not appealing in the way they would be if you were regressing into old behaviors. You wouldn't want the old relationship you had, nor would you want to participate at work the way you used to.

You may have to take my word on this for now, and trust the process, but I have seen people in similar situations as yourself. They have emerged much stronger than they ever thought was possible. They look back and are glad that things fell apart, for it allowed them to become a more expansive, more effective, more beautiful version of themselves.

Believe it or not, they even ask for another round of this sort of growth. They ask to be stripped away of even more of what no longer serves them, because they know that what will emerge will be even better. They start to trust in the process of personal transformation. They let it work them over. They get wrung out, shaken up, fluffed out, and left to dry in the sun. They emerge smelling sweeter, feeling warmer, and looking brighter. Hang on—because you are right there with them!

Fondly yours,
David

Dear Chloe,

I know that you are the one who usually takes care of everything. You are the capable one in your family and at work. You are strong, and that's great, but it has consistently put you in the position of being responsible. I hear you, it's a drag. When others underperform, you step in to take care of it. Why? Because you can.

I agree that it is not fair to have to bear the responsibility at work. I guess this comes with being super capable and effective. I also hear how you resent having to do everything at home while your partner can't carry his end of the load. I don't blame you. It is unfair.

You also play a certain score-keeping game with those around you, counting how many times you do something for them versus how little they do for you. What do you get from this score keeping? Perhaps you track how much you have been wronged, so that you can calculate how many times you have given more than your share. The bad news is that there will be no reward given for those who have done way more for others. No referee is going to come in and give the other person a penalty for not carrying their weight. There is no "people did nothing for you" trophy.

One option for you would be to withhold. You could be less loving, less capable, and let things slide. If the ledger has been unbalanced in your relationships, then you could reduce your side. This might work for a while, but playing takeaway usually doesn't end up fixing much of anything in the long run. Instead, withholding goes against your capable and loving nature and ends up leaving you even more resentful.

Perhaps we could instead look together at what you can control in this situation. I want us to look at what it means to be responsible, and perhaps refine and change its meaning for you. Old programming suggests that being responsible means bearing burdens, owning failures, and dealing with punishments when things go wrong. It is an old paradigm of "taking one for the team." Responsibility has been about sacrifice. No wonder those, like you, who bear it end up feeling resentful.

A new way of looking at responsibility is to see it as an opportunity. Responsibility is just what it sounds like: response plus ability. You have the ability to respond. When a situation arises, you know how to skillfully provide what is needed in each moment. Having this ability is a true gift. It is part of what you are here to offer the world. Instead of shrinking from your ability to respond, perhaps we can find a way to make it a joyful, artful way of giving your love.

Increasing your willingness to be responsible would be the first step. It would reduce your resentment. You would have to own your abilities and recognize that many of those around you do not have the same capacity. There will be times when you will be the smartest one in the room, the strongest emotionally, the bigger person who has to contain a situation while the other throws a tantrum. This comes with being able to respond.

I think of Harry Potter in this sort of situation. In J. K. Rowling's books there are Wizards and Muggles. The Wizards have a certain ability that the Muggles do not. The Wizards are capable in many ways, while the Muggles are the "normies" of society. We love the Muggles. They are great in their own way. Yet the main rule of being a Wizard is not to practice magic in front of a Muggle. It scares them and then they attack you. The responsibility is on the part of the Wizard to manage things capably and leave the Muggles none the wiser.

Chloe, whether or not you resent being a Wizard, these are the rules. Breaking them just causes you more pain. At some point, when we have more capacity in a certain situation, we need to joyfully own our abilities. It usually won't be a balanced and even exchange, and your relationship ledger may look quite unfair. Yet if you take a broader view, you might see that the score eventually evens out. What you give, you receive back threefold in many other ways.

Instead of playing tit for tat at work and at home, I encourage you to see the greater benefits of giving your gifts freely while trusting that you will receive your share back somehow.

It is giving without expectation of receiving that releases the resentment. The joy comes in giving what you have. If you are more able to listen to others than they are to you, then go ahead and listen to them without expecting them to do much in return. Listen to them until you start to get a little tired. Then set your boundaries. Stop listening and move on to the next thing. Now, you don't have to go without being listened to yourself. Instead of expecting that the other person will listen to you back, go out and find someone who has the capability to listen to you. There is no reason for you to go without. Just be clear about where you get your needs met.

Let's set your partner up for success. If listening is not their strong suit, then find your listening elsewhere with friends. Make the marriage about companionship, or love, or really great co-parenting. The key is to work with what you have and make it the best it can be.

I hear from many people who resent having to be the one who does the heavy lifting in their relationship. They don't want the responsibility of making their marriage better. Instead they expect their partner to do their share. This would be ideal if the partner could, but often it is the one who is more able to respond who bears the burden of creating and leading marital growth. It's up to you. It's your marriage. Make it the best it can be for you. Be the change that you want to see in your marriage.

Responsibility ain't so bad. Give it a try. At least shift the way you think about it to embrace your ability to respond. Being a leader at home and at work might be something that brings you joy and purpose. Please remember that being responsible does not mean you have to go without. You can find your connection and fulfillment in so many ways, often from unlikely sources. Many of us wish things were different and complain about it. Yet it will be your willingness to take on responsibility that will make all the difference.

Fondly yours,
David

Dear Frank: Confusion Sandwich

Dear Frank,

I am glad that I have a chance to write to you. Our sessions go by quickly, and are so filled with information, that I do not often have a chance to fully speak to what you share with me. My job, as I humbly see it, is to help you gain insight into yourself, and find deeper meaning and purpose in your relationships. Yet with all that you have going on, it has been difficult for us to go there. We spend more time unraveling your confusing thoughts. My hope is that in this letter I can help you undo some misunderstandings you have about yourself, and about the world.

Like many people, you have what I call a confusion sandwich. This is where a misunderstanding grows out of an already faulty belief and then further builds on itself. For example, you grew up in an atmosphere in which there was a high level of competition. People were always vying to get ahead and find every little advantage to be the best at school, at work, or socially. Their need for competition grew from an existing collective belief that there is not enough to go around, that if they do not compete they will fall behind and be left with nothing. Perhaps there are degrees of truth to these beliefs, but what occurred for you is that from these beliefs about competition and scarcity, you developed misunderstandings about your worth.

Because most of us do not win at everything, you have believed for so long that you were not good enough to have what you wanted. You thought that because you were not the best in school, did not have the best job, and struggled at times socially, that you were unworthy, and did not deserve to have what you wanted. This faulty belief springs from the already existing misunderstandings that you need to compete for everything and that resources are scarce. Regardless of how true any of these beliefs are, you can see how there are layers of convictions that build on one another and create an entrenched worldview.

Our work together, Frank, has only allowed us to get to some top layer beliefs, as your mind jumps from topic to topic. You are often off to the next subject before we have a chance to unpack, for example, this belief that you are not good enough. Because it is so layered, you feel stuck in a world that has limiting belief piled on top of limiting belief. I am here to tell you that these beliefs can be undone and that you can start to have new experiences in life if you are open to receiving them.

We need to address this confusion sandwich first. Its special sauce is judgment. When we don't understand something that bothers us, what most of us do is start judging it. Frank, because you didn't understand why you kept falling short in the various competitions of who gets better grades, who is more popular, and eventually who has the better job and makes more money, you chose to judge that you were not good enough. Rather than understanding that the competition was a faulty construct in the first place, you blamed yourself. Had people shared resources, then perhaps there would be enough to go around, and competition would be obsolete. Yet you bought into the collective scarcity picture and tried your best to compete in realms in which you had massive disadvantages. When you fell behind, you judged yourself as being faulty. This has led to a gross misunderstanding about who you are.

Judgments hold together the confusion sandwich and keep you from knowing yourself. Once you start judging something, your relationship with it ends. For instance, if I was looking at an abstract piece of art and trying to make sense of it, I might notice how it made me feel and venture some guesses as to what the artist was trying to convey. Yet the second I say to myself, "This is weird. I don't like it," my relationship with the artwork ends, and any further inquiry ceases. Similarly, when we look at ourselves, our judgments prevent any chance for new perspectives.

Once we are locked out of self-inquiry, the confusion sandwich starts to go stale. Our self-judgment turns to hatred. We know something hurts inside, and that there is a lie we can't quite understand.

Because any investigation is prevented by self-judgment, we start subtly hating ourselves. Our confusion mixes with self-hatred, and it is this toxic mix that is at the root of most human suffering.

Instead of bouncing from topic to topic in our sessions, Frank, perhaps we could peek inside and find something useful. Perhaps you could forgive yourself for having believed for so long that you are not good enough. You might forgive yourself for thinking that you are not good enough, that there is no hope, that you are not loved, that nobody can help you, that you are foolish, that this world does not care for you, and that you don't deserve to be happy. You could create your own list of faulty beliefs about yourself and the world and start to release them.

What I find compelling in this process is that you are forgiving yourself for having believed something wrong. You don't have to forgive yourself for how you acted, or who you have been, but simply for having held faulty assumptions. I find this to be a very compassionate approach to our healing, since who among us hasn't believed something for a long time that we later learned was incorrect?

We have all been wrong in our convictions at some point. Forgiving yourself for having faulty beliefs is a great step toward ending confusion. You might even find that your truth is paradoxical compared to what you have previously believed. You might, in fact, actually be good enough to have what you want. There might be plenty to go around, and no need for competition in your world. As long as you keep eating that confusion sandwich, you stay stuck in old fears. Perhaps now, instead, is the time for a truth burger!

Fondly yours,
David

Dear Julia: The Wisdom to Know the Difference

Dear Julia,

You shrug your shoulders and say, "I don't know" when asked how you might do something to alleviate your worry. I believe you. You feel like it is impossible to make things more peaceful at home. Your adult children are fighting and won't talk with one another, and your marriage leaves you feeling neglected. To your credit, you have a powerful intellect and you are able to analyze the situation. Yet your intellect works against you when you are unable to take action.

It is called paralysis by analysis. You work yourself up by turning the problem over and over in your head. You perseverate to a point where your anxiety starts to spike and you have the occasional panic attack. This is common for people who care. They worry about those they love, and it becomes difficult when they see their loved ones struggle.

When I ask what you might do to help your daughter feel more independent, or to fix your marriage, you do the same old shrug. It indicates a felt sense of helplessness. You don't know what to do. I don't mind listening to your struggles and complaints, but I also want to find a way for you to feel empowered to do something about them. This, I believe, will reduce your anxiety.

From a psychological perspective, I think that the Serenity Prayer has good applications here. Originally authored by the American theologian Reinhold Niebuhr, the prayer goes as follows:

God, grant me the serenity to accept the things I cannot change,
Courage to change the things I can,
And wisdom to know the difference.[6]

If we find the courage to change the things we can, then perhaps we will feel more effective in our lives. Even if our efforts don't end up making a difference, we might still feel better about ourselves if we have the courage to try. When problems come our way (and being human, life can be full of endless "problems"), our ability to know that we have the inherent capacity to change our conditions allows for greater psychological well-being. Just trying helps.

Julia, when you shrug your shoulders, you are effectively saying to yourself, "I can't change the conditions in my life." If that is indeed the case, and you truly can't change a particular situation, then we should work on serenity to accept your situation as it is. However, I do not believe that you would be complaining about the conditions of your home life unless you knew somewhere inside of you that change is possible. I think it bothers you so much because you know that at some level you have the power and ability to transform what is bothering you. You just need help figuring out how.

That is where wisdom comes in. The wisdom to know the difference between whether your situation is one that requires serenity or courage is the key to this prayer. It takes wisdom to know what is required in various situations. I call this approach skillful means. When we can ascertain how to approach a problem, and we do so mindfully and with the appropriate tenor, then we are employing skillful means. Instead of using analysis to dwell on problems, let's use it to determine how to best approach changing the situation.

Julia, I ask you to call upon skillful means for those situations in your life that cause you stress. First employ your wisdom to know whether the situation is one in which you can do something to make a difference. If it is, then you must become willing to do something. Look back over what you've tried before that has had some success. Even if that prior approach stopped working, perhaps you could revisit what did work. See how you might update your interactions so that they reflect the sort of tone you want in your life.

On the other hand, if you assess the situation and see that certain aspects are beyond your control, then we need to focus on acceptance. Acceptance is different from giving up, or allowing bad things to continue. If your adult daughter is making self-destructive choices, there might only be so much you can do. Acceptance, however, might allow you to find serenity within the current unmovable situation.

Your situation, in my opinion, however, is movable. There are things that you can do to change the conditions at home. Perhaps you can bond with your daughter in her love of country music, or take your son, who dreams of being a chef, to some cooking classes. Most people feel that they are doing everything they can, but with a bit of reflection, dialogue, and imagination, they often find that they are not even doing half of what is possible. Try everything that you can to change things in your life. Be creative, be courageous, summon the warrior of love within you, and speak your truth. Whatever you do, try to find a way to give it your all. If you try everything and the situation is still the same, then at least you will know that you did everything you could.

Couples who want to divorce benefit from this sort of approach. When they know that they have tried everything to fix their marriage, then it is easier to walk away. Yet, like most of us, they usually haven't done everything possible. Your marriage, like many others, suffers from a failure of imagination. You act as if you need to summon the serenity to accept the marriage as it is, yet in reality you need to find the courage to change what you can! You are not using your wisdom, which would know that this relationship is one in which you have tremendous power to make a difference. Might you find a time to go for regular walks with your husband, or let him know more about the new work you're doing at the botanical garden? Through such examples of skillful means, you can start creating a feeling in the marriage that reflects your highest ideals and your deepest love.

I am with you in this. Summoning courage and using wisdom is not an easy road, but it is the mature path. Being an adult means taking responsibility for what is in front of us. It means being skillful even when we feel mistreated. Instead of shrugging, I encourage you to flex your muscles!

Fondly yours,
David

PART X

The Deeper Work

DEPTH WORK IN THERAPY is an entirely different process. It involves going to the places within us that most of us generally avoid. Therapy typically involves alleviating pain, solving problems, and finding new meaning. Yet, for some, personal growth work can involve looking more deeply into who we are; although most of us run from deeper pains, there are a select few people who go toward what hurts.

When clients are able to look within and access their depth, it changes the therapeutic process into one of exploration and discovery. A lot of our inner world is not mapped out, so the therapeutic work ends up looking more like piecing together a puzzle in the dark. We get glimpses of what our inner lives are like through dreams or fleeting thoughts. It is usually seen out of the corner of our mind's eye, but we can begin a process of mapping out what our inner self looks like.

Often in the depths we find shadowy aspects of ourselves that have been splintered off. We discover the opposite of who we have thought ourselves to be. For instance, if I consider myself a kind and compassionate person, I might find, through depth work, that there are aspects of me living down there that are cruel and withholding, which need transformation. Being able to look at these parts is like seeing in the dark. It involves being open to the mysteries that lie within us.

I love doing this deeper work with people because there is often treasure in these deeper parts of us. Though it might not feel comfortable to look within, there is often great reward in the form of increased power, ability, or strength.

The letters that follow are to people who are considering deeper work, or who have been involved in their own growth and development for some time. The letters address what it is like to be a sensitive person in this world, and how to develop internal structure in the places within that lack formation. Using metaphor, story, and creative visualization, the goal is to map out a bit more detail describing what is happening inside of them.

Dear Karen: Look Inside Yourself

Dear Karen,

It is so painful to watch you search endlessly outside yourself. You have been searching for relationships, classes, teachers, activities, books, travel or anything external to give your life meaning and fulfilment. Look inside yourself instead! I am writing to encourage you to cultivate your awareness of what we might call the inner plains within you. There is a vast world that exists within. We could imagine a landscape of various climates and terrains, where the laws of physics that rule our outer world cease to exist. Perhaps gravity and music and emotion flow in different ways. Maybe communication happens differently.

Maybe we could even imagine a multifaceted jewel inside your heart. There we would find the many faces of who you are as a complex being. We would see a range of personal and spiritual expression. Perhaps multiple histories and narratives exist in each face of this jewel … endless permutations of your humanity.

When I meet with you, I imagine that I see these inner planes. I hear from the variety of self-expressions that emanate from this jewel deep in your heart. There are treasures within you. Yet in our sessions, all you report seeing is your outer reality. You tell me of disappointments and empty pursuits. You describe in great detail your anxiety and the panic that comes with the unknown: the fear of being on stage as a sales trainer and presenting at industry conferences, and the misery of imagining what others are thinking about you.

These are your realities, so I meet you there. Your consciousness lives in this day-to-day world of angst. I can be with you in this reality. I don't mind it too much. Yet I also long for you to see what is inside of you—to be in touch with the inner plains of existence. My hunch is that if you get in touch with what's inside, you will find great relief from the worldly stresses you endure.

Somehow, though, you do manage to glimpse that world now and again. Occasionally you will tell me of a fantastic dream, or how a novel you are reading stirred something within. Those are lovely moments; yet quickly the pain of work politics or family dynamics eclipses the fleeting pleasure of the heart.

I am not sure what I can do to get you to look inside. I want to help you develop an inner vision, yet you suffer from what we might call head-blindness. This inability to see more than your outer reality is a sort of delusional hypnosis that humanity faces. It is as if we are all in a collective trance, having been lured away from the worlds inside of us into an illusory outer reality. Instead of staying head-blind, we have to open an inner vision and learn to start seeing inside ourselves.

We must turn inward and find the resources within us to sustain a life. Often something has to break open within us so that we can see the treasures that lie within. I don't know of another way to end this collective delusional trance for you. Usually something painful enough happens that we are forced to seek refuge within our own hearts. Gently, every time we meet, Karen, I pull you there: there, into your own heart.

I invite you to spend more time within. To take a seat and see what emerges. Take a breath and be inside yourself for a moment. Look around. Tell me what you see. I am interested.

Fondly yours,
David

Dear Nia: How to Be Sensitive in This World

Dear Nia,

Human beings are so good at letting us down. They neglect us inadvertently or even intentionally. They talk about themselves and don't listen. They say they'll be there, but then leave. Being close to others starts to hurt as they pull and push on us, and play out their pain and struggles in the relationship.

If you were raised by humans, then chances are you were neglected in some way. I don't know exactly why it is this way. Perhaps it is some grand design; it is common for people to feel not fully cared for growing up. Though you were raised by solid, stable, and well-meaning parents, Nia, through no fault of their own, they let you down. Yes, they raised you and your sister to be healthy, productive members of society; yet they also made you feel less certain of yourself. They were busy and couldn't consistently attend to your needs. They became frustrated as you became more demanding, and made you feel foolish for needing more. They told you that you were too sensitive and that you should appreciate everything you have ... and you believed them. You became ashamed of how sensitive you were, and how deeply you could feel, and that shame continues to this day.

I get that it can be rough to be a sensitive person in this world. It doesn't take much to make you feel pretty horrible. So easily can other human beings be cruel, careless, and dismissive with your heart. Being an emotional person can lead to being more easily wounded. Yet the answer is not to close up, or shut down your sensitivity, but to better understand how to be intimate with others while still protecting yourself.

The term "highly sensitive person" was coined in the mid-1990s by psychologists Elaine Aron and her husband Arthur Aron. It refers to a type of person who has a hypersensitivity to the external world, a greater expansiveness of thinking, and who feels more deeply. A highly sensitive person is impacted by the world in ways that may become confusing. You, dear Nia, are likely a highly sensitive person, and it may take a little extra care in order for you to navigate what life throws your way.

One way to do this is to better understand where you stop and other people start. When we are close to others, we get sort of commingled. It can be hard to tell who is who. If the other person starts to feel a bit depressed, then you might become a bit blue. If your partner is an anxious traveler, then you might start to worry more when on vacation together. There can be confusion as to which emotional and mental material is yours and which belongs to the other. As a result, we need emotional and psychic boundaries in order to sustain closeness.

It feels good to merge and connect with other people. A lot of people love "losing themselves" in the other person. They get lost in the other person's eyes, or feel swept away into an ecstatic coming together. This is wonderful, and one of the higher experiences of human love. In order to sustain it you would need to know how to differentiate yourself from the other person. You would have to find a sense of "me" in the "we."

Merging and deeply connecting with others while maintaining a sense of who you are is only possible when you can distinguish what is you from what is not you. There is a subtle psychic phenomenon in which an exchange of thoughts and feelings mix together and form a greater whole. American psychiatrist Murray Bowen called it the undifferentiated family ego mass. It describes a "conglomerate emotional oneness that exists in all levels of intensity."[7] On one level each person is an individual, but on another subterranean level, the core central group is as one.

It makes me think of the aspen trees that can live for thousands of years as a colony connected by their roots. There are parent trees that stem off and sprout other trees. In a way they are each separate trees, living and dying, but the system is connected at the roots as one organism. Families and close relationships can feel like this as well. Rather than simply being a tree, however, the highly sensitive person tunes into the overall root system and senses what is happening for the other trees. This is a great asset when a situation calls for empathy or deep compassion. It helps us understand how we are connected to one another. Yet when we don't nourish our own roots, and don't reach for the sun ourselves, then we wither.

This level of sensitivity to others is also called being an empath. An empath is really able to tune into other people and know more deeply what is going on for them. It can be wonderful to connect to others that way, and they often feel deeply listened to and cared for. Yet when someone is that empathic and sensitive, the connection can cause many of the problems that you have been expressing. The symptoms I hear you talk about are common among highly sensitive individuals and empaths.

Confusion in relationships, emoting too easily and at inappropriate moments, overwhelming negativity, difficulties in crowds, being ashamed of feeling too deeply, coping by pretending to be aloof or cool, feeling insecure, excessive self-blame, heightened levels of fear and anxiety, and not tolerating pain very well are just a few symptoms of being sensitive in this world. You describe feeling like a dumping ground for the problems of those around you, and don't know how to prevent this from happening. It has been a painful experience, and you have been coping by withdrawing.

Taking up more space in your own life will help counteract these symptoms, Nia. There needs to be more of you in your life. In other words, when you are faced with a situation in which you are feeling what everyone else is feeling, start to tune into what is really going on for you. Instead of listening to others and being their dumping ground, tell them what is happening in your life. They might not listen very well, but at least there will be less room for them to simply vent. The key is to crowd out the disrupting external stimuli with more of your own thoughts, feelings, and desires. Instead of being an empty vessel that gets filled by the world, become filled with yourself.

Obviously this is not being full of yourself in an egotistical or selfish way, but in a way that tends to your own roots, trunk, limbs, leaves, and flowers. This creates more balance and allows for smoother relationships. It creates appropriate boundaries so that it is easier to maintain closeness in relationships.

Do not lose your sensitivity, however. It is one of your greatest gifts. It is okay to feel deeply and express what lies in your heart. The world can make it tough for those who do so; but if you carefully navigate it by distinguishing and differentiating who you are, and not letting the world fill you in, then you will bring those gifts to others. You will find the ability to touch, move, and inspire those around you very deeply.

Fondly yours,
David

Dear Mark,

You have signed up for the advanced class. For one reason or another, you have taken on a level of personal growth and looking inward that typically exceeds the range of what psychotherapy covers. Generally, we address the alleviation of symptoms and the enhancement of relationships. We help people look into themselves and better understand who they are. Yet we often do not work at the deep level of internal restructuring, which you seem to be doing.

Swiss psychoanalyst and pioneer Carl Jung was onto something when he took a much more penetrating and symbolic look at our inner lives. He understood that the relationships between various aspects of ourselves either caused harmony or distress, depending on how we related to them. He worked at the level of archetypes, which are universal characters that reside in the psyche, constituting a deep, emotional sense of who we are.

Today's therapists borrow a lot from Jung, but it is often difficult to put his work into practice. Addressing the hidden archetypes of the patient is difficult because it is hard to know what to do with them once they are discovered. Many therapists relate to the archetypal parts on a more cerebral level. They talk *about* the archetypes rather than working directly with them to transform them. This is mainly because most of us do not know what to do when we get to the archetypal level. The level is buried and not well mapped out. Instead of fumbling around in the dark of the psyche, therapists usually stay on a more cognitive and well-worn path.

Yet where we have been able to go in our work together, Mark, is toward those hidden depths. We have been mapping out a structure within you where there was not one before. I know we have talked a little bit about internal structure, but I wanted to expand on what this means when it comes to your growth and healing. Just like a building that has a foundation and framework to hold up its structure, so, too, do our inner lives have a certain form. Without a strong foundation of self, we cannot hold the weight of any personal development. Our inner lives have a sort of blueprint or map. Once we start looking inside, we might find areas that are built up and developed while others are unformed and lacking development.

For instance, you might be very disciplined when it comes to your job. You have a strong sense of ethics and integrity with your work. Giving presentations, speeches, and handling pressured decision-making are skills you have developed over the years. In other words, you may really know who you are in your work life. Yet when it comes to home life, you might be making it up as you go along. You say one thing and do another. You may have no real vision or mission when it comes to your relationship. Instead of stepping up when it is most needed, you hide and withdraw. Though in your work you have strong boundaries, at home they are diffuse. The idea here is that for one reason or another, your inner self at home, your archetypal lover, is underdeveloped, while your inner worker, your archetypal warrior or king, has much more structure.

Where most people get stuck is that they keep building up their strong aspects while further neglecting their undeveloped parts. Our work has been to go toward what is weak and work to build strength there. Like a first responder running toward danger, you have taken on a willingness to go toward what hurts rather than running screaming from it like most of us usually do. Instead of building on your strengths, we have had the opportunity to look at your shadowy weaknesses that quietly plague you.

You have clear strengths when it comes to work and leadership. You are a great father, friend, and boss. People around you feel motivated. The internal structure of the king archetype is strong. Yet when it comes to the lover archetype, you have become painfully aware that you lack integrity. There is little development in that part of you. Without boundaries, this part of you is a morass of unformed machinations and deceptions. At work, your word is your bond. In your love life you say one thing and do another. At the office there is follow-through. At home you leave things undone.

I say all of this to you not from a place of judgment. Actually, as you have found, it has been a relief to have this spoken out loud. These are things you already know about yourself; they have just lived in the blind spots of your underdeveloped inner self. Your willingness to start to look at these areas is truly brave and inspiring. It speaks to your character. Yet now that we know where the weaknesses lie, our work to develop structure there begins.

In order to build strength, you need to adjust the foundation of who you are. You need to step out of old convictions and values that no longer serve you and embrace what might allow for even more growth and development. This sort of foundation change can be tremendously upsetting, as you have experienced. It disrupts everything we have known. Yet unearthing the misconceptions and replacing them with truth becomes a much-needed relief. Let's look at your core foundational beliefs regarding love.

An old outworn sense of entitlement drives many of your actions. Growing up as a golden child in your family, you took on the misconception that you did not have to do much in order to be loved. You could even act out and be loved. Your mother, in particular, turned a blind eye to your faults. While this was good for your self-esteem, it didn't give you a realistic sense of how your actions impacted others. You were living with this misconception that you could do anything and people would still love you. The side effect was that you didn't feel as close to others. It didn't feel like they really knew you and understood you. An imposter syndrome was born in that you could look good and charm others while they would never know the real you. It was a buried loneliness that created an unformed internal structure around love and intimacy.

Since we have discovered that these are some of your core foundational misconceptions, we are now able to release and undo them. The work of noticing these misconstructions and not employing them has begun. When you recognize the tendency to behave in an inauthentic way, you are now able to catch yourself and start telling your truth to those you love. We are slowly building the structure of what it takes to hold love. This is not just a set of new behaviors; rather, you are becoming more grounded in honesty and integrity in your love life. You are embodying the internal qualities of a loving partner. Instead of living in the old structure of entitlement and dishonesty, you know what it means to share who you truly are.

I see this transformation as truly sacred. It is the unearthing of your truth so that you can live it. Whereas before you were living the misunderstandings and lies transmitted to you while growing up, now you have the chance to ground your life in your deepest truth. When you are living your truth, anything is possible.

Fondly yours,
David

Dear Michelle: Change Your Mind

Dear Michelle,

I have come to learn how quick your mind is. It can spin a hundred different interpretations around a single event. It can make sense of almost every problem. This is a great trait, but it is a lot of work. Your countless, well-crafted solutions do everything to alter deeply painful experiences so that they come out looking like gold. Yet it pains me to say that it often feels like fool's gold. I can feel how stuck you are underneath your analysis. Your charm and grace keep others from seeing it, but in the sacred space of therapy, your dystopian worldview reveals itself.

I think of the words of twentieth-century Austrian poet Rainer Maria Rilke when he says, "The work of the eyes is done. Go now and do the heart-work on the images imprisoned within you."[8]

I hear him telling us that the work of generating analytical answers is done. It's now time for you to go to work on the symbolic images in your mind that limit you. Words only go so far. We need to address the pictures in your mind's eye. For, you see, mental image pictures shape our reality. They are the pictures that rise up in our imagination and tell us about the world.

For instance, if I tell you that I was at the beach, you may instantly conjure up a picture in your mind of a beach. I don't have to describe the sun, surf, and sand because a picture tells a thousand words. Telling you that I was at the beach might bring up feelings that you have about the beach. These feelings might be very different from those evoked if I told you I was at a mall parking lot, which elicits a whole other set of mental image pictures. Any sort of communication or story involves these scenes in our mind, or mental image pictures. If at the beach I told you that I saw a figure walking along the shore from far away, and that as she got closer, I started to recognize her, you likely are already forming a picture in your mind of this scene.

Our minds create our reality through these internal scenes.

A big part of therapy is getting to know another person and understanding how they see the world. To do so, I need to know more about the core pictures that shape your reality. Over the time of us meeting, Michelle, I have begun to see the pictures through which you see the world. Your world centers around hard work and effort. You describe a scene from your youth in which you struggled mightily to seek a place on your soccer team and eventually earned success. I can see the blue first-place ribbon and trophy that you described winning in a tournament when you were 11 years old. A lot of your current reality of success and determination comes from that core memory. You gleaned from that experience that if you work really hard, you will achieve good outcomes.

Today that image still runs your life. The dirt and sweat from the soccer jersey of that 11- year-old still is with you today. Rather than finding ease and effortless receiving in your life, you come back to that old picture of effort and reward. You take on any problem you face from that picture. Yet that approach is no longer working very well. The old picture of struggle does not serve you. It is outworn and outdated. My job is to help you leave that old picture and step into new ones that better serve you.

In some way it feels like my job is that of the shaman in the invisible ships story. This is the story about Christopher Columbus (or Captain Cook, or Magellan, depending on the version of the story) arriving in the new world. The story is that the native people could not see the huge ships off shore because the ships were so alien to their experience. Even though the ships were a thousand yards away, their brains could not register what their eyes were seeing because it was so out of their existing picture of reality. The local shaman saw that there was something blocking the waves in a certain part of the sea and was able to eventually see the ships and describe them to the locals. The locals could then see the ships as the shaman helped them open their eyes to seeing something new for the first time.

The truth of this story is debatable. However, it serves here as a good metaphor when we think of how the existing pictures in our mind limit us from experiencing the world in a new way. Michelle, if you were to let go of the old core picture that says it is effort that gets you the trophy, then you might be able to step into a new picture that could be about effortlessness and joyous receiving.

Changing the way we look at the world is no easy task for an adult. When we were younger, we were more open to looking at the world in new ways. We experienced it anew each day. As we get older, we start to focus on making sense of the world rather than experiencing it. If you give a baby a set of keys, he often plays with them as if they are fun, magic toys. To us, they are just keys; to the baby they are something new and jingly.

It is similar to the way we might look at the moon. We know a lot about the moon without actually looking at it. We know it's about 240,000 miles away, that it waxes and wanes, and that the light coming from it is not its own but merely the reflection of the sun. Understanding the moon might help explain what we're looking at, but it keeps us from truly seeing the moon.

Michelle, can we make room for new possibilities? To do this, we need to create new pictures in your mind about who you are and what is possible in your life. This process is called visualization. Athletes do this when they imagine themselves scoring a goal before the match. People use this process when they create vision boards to gain clarity on what they want to create in their lives. The key is to find the images for which you have a great affinity.

I know you are attached to the vision of the 11-year-old winning the trophy after hard work, but I don't think you have an affinity for it any longer. Perhaps you might be more fond of a new vision. One that has bold colors and expansive horizons. Something that more accurately reflects your core values and deepest truths. The key will be to clarify in your mind what that image looks like. Can you see it clearly and give it details? The more you see yourself in a new picture, the clearer it might become, and the more easily you might step out of the old and into the new. I look forward to helping you step out of those old versions of reality and into something that more readily suits the current you.

Fondly yours,
David

PART XI
Developing Mastery

FOR THE MORE ADVANCED aspirants among us, the path of personal growth leads toward mastery. There are those who really want to take on their personal growth and development so that it becomes the central theme in their life. They might still enjoy a family and career, they might be raising children or in a satisfying relationship, but they put their personal growth and development at the forefront. These people find satisfaction in what comes with being completely responsible for their own life. For some it is a grueling path, and for others it takes tremendous time; ultimately, these folks are looking for support and information on the more esoteric, less traveled, aspects of life.

While this material may not be for everyone, it does speak to some general themes such as being able to see the bigger picture in one's life, and embracing what is, rather than going into the type of resistance and complaining that most of us do. By seeing a larger framework, we start to see that our psychological and emotional lives are governed by more than just our mindset. We see that we are connected to a global community that is going through its own changes. Seeing a larger framework allows those developing personal mastery to embrace the circumstances in their lives and work more deeply to create positive change.

Whereas some of us stay at the level of making sense of our experiences, and trying to alter our behavior to better suit our goals, those who have prioritized their personal growth tend to need to work more deeply on the core aspects that shape their reality. They are looking for more foundational and expansive shifts in who they are. It is an exciting undertaking to work at this level, but it is not for everyone.

These letters are to clients who are working to master who they are. These letters encourage them to stop resisting the circumstances in their lives and instead start working with them. They encourage these clients to expand to new ways of working, including learning how to create a sacred space that can support them in their endeavors. I encourage you to take whatever you find useful in these following letters. My hope is that you might find a little something that can help you on your way.

Dear Bobbie: Embrace What Is

Dear Bobbie,

Have you heard the story of the monk who was being chased by a tiger? The monk was walking through a forest when a tiger crept upon him and began chasing him. The monk ran for his life through the forest with the tiger at his heels. He got to a clearing at the edge of the forest and found himself backed up against a thousand-foot cliff. If he fell off the cliff, he would surely perish. If the tiger got hold of him, he would be toast. Either way he was in trouble.

As the monk backed toward the edge of the cliff, the tiger ready to pounce, he spotted a wild strawberry bush on the cliff's edge. Growing on this bush was the most beautiful, fresh, ripe strawberry the monk had ever seen. He reached for the strawberry, picked it, and savored it. He exclaimed, "This lovely strawberry, how sweet it tastes!"

This is a story from Zen Buddhism that obviously seems like a bit of an exaggeration. How could anyone, when faced with such terrifying consequences as a tiger or a cliff, focus on the strawberry bush, let alone have the presence of mind to enjoy a strawberry? Perhaps he had developed a sensibility that found the beauty in life in all circumstances. Perhaps he had learned lessons of impermanence, and made a practice of savoring life. There are various interpretations of the tale. Yet based on our recent sessions, Bobbie, I think that what is most salient for you is the monk's ability to embrace what is.

Instead of wishing his circumstances were different, our monk embraces what he is facing. This allows him to see the bush. If he wished that there was no tiger or cliff, then he presumably would not see the strawberry since his mind would be elsewhere. It would be understandable if he resented his precarious situation. I would not blame him if he wished he was back at the monastery, or even that he never joined the monastery in the first place. Those would be normal reactions.

Here's another example: I get a flat tire and pull over to the side of the road. I most certainly would start wishing this wasn't happening. I might even kick myself for not fixing my spare. I could sit there on the side of the road all afternoon, cursing the situation or blaming myself. I could ruminate on how I should have listened to my father who always told me to have a full-sized spare in the trunk. Yet at some point I would need to embrace what is, and do something about the tire.

By acknowledging the situation as it is, I become more empowered. I can take action. The monk chooses to eat a strawberry. I can choose to get the tire changed. Both seem like pretty good choices considering the varying severity of the situations! Even if you don't like your situation in life, you open up new possibilities when you embrace it. In a way you are choosing to live in what is, rather than wishing it was otherwise.

Bobbie, you are up against some pretty challenging life situations. You have your own cliffs and tigers. You have been managing chronic health issues, caring for your aging father, dealing with stress at home, and working at a job that has a demanding climate. I understand how you feel regularly defeated. Yet it is precisely in these situations where we benefit from embracing the conditions and working with them. Choose your life circumstances as they are even if you don't like them. Even if your heart is broken, embrace what is, so that you can become creative again.

Once the monk accepts his fate, he sees the strawberry. Once I stop throwing a tantrum about my flat tire, I go about fixing it. Once you embrace your life's situation, you can take steps to find creative solutions. You can use your inventiveness, your zest for life, your ability to find humor and amusement in the strangest moments, to lift yourself up. It is a more powerful stance than wishing it was otherwise or resisting the state of affairs.

Most people complain and resist instead of choose and embrace. They get something out of a "life sucks" approach. It serves them in some roundabout way to complain about their circumstances and resist life. Just like building a dam in a stream, resisting life blocks its progression. It increases the volume of distress on its upstream bank. What you resist persists. When you fight against the circumstances in your life, they only increase. When you complain about and refuse to accept your situation, you only get handed more of it. This is one of life's cruel jokes, and the only way out is to end the war within yourself.

In a subtle way, Bobbie, you are at war inside. It might be hard to admit it, but there is a battle going on within you against your own life. It comes from a good place. You have high standards and ideals, and a pure vision of how you want your life to be. You have been disappointed that many of your dreams have not been realized, and you have become quietly angry about it. You have said to me on many occasions, "This is not how it should be." I feel you when you say that. I feel the sadness and hurt under the angry resistance. I feel the fervent sorrow underneath the holy war you wage against your life. You have been telling life how it should be rather than connecting to it.

Instead of indulging the urge to defy and push back, I respectfully invite you to practice nonresistance. When you find something you don't like inside yourself, rather than condemn it, I encourage you to investigate and connect with it. My hunch is that when you stop resisting, and instead work with what is, you might find a new power to change what is hurting you. You might find real peace.

I see my role in this as embodying the embrace. I will be here to hold space for you for whatever you bring. While I might not always "feel bad" for you when you are complaining, I will most certainly investigate with compassionate curiosity what is going on for you. My aim is that my nonresistance will rub off, and that you will start approaching your own life similarly. When you go to war with yourself, I'll be a peacekeeper. When all you can see are the cliffs and tigers, I'll help you find the strawberries.

Fondly yours,
David

Dear Patricia: See the Bigger Picture

Dear Patricia,

The cup of tea that you drink each time we meet is said to have been made by more than 50 people. The tea leaf growers, harvesters, transporters, packagers, along with the people who made and delivered your mug, and delivered your water so that you can brew it, have helped bring you this cup of tea. While it is normal to feel that you alone are brewing your tea, you risk becoming myopic if you are not aware of the number of people who have helped make that cup of tea possible. Sometimes all that we see is our own lives in front of us. It can be difficult to be aware of the myriad connections that sustain us.

Similarly in your own life, when you tell me about recently feeling very unsure of yourself, that your normal confidence has faded, and that you have started to feel increasingly anxious, you are reporting to me symptoms that are like that cup of tea. You think that you alone have contributed to the change in your confidence, and that something you have done must have caused increased doubt to creep in. Yet many people and circumstances have gone into creating this unsettling change in who you are. I think that Psychology gets it wrong when we think that the individual alone is responsible for their social or emotional changes. I think it helps to instead see how our states of mind are impacted by the collective consciousness endlessly shifting and evolving beneath our awareness.

When we embrace our interconnectedness, we take steps to understand who we are. Certainly we each have our own life experiences, yet there is a general collective ego mass that regularly impacts us. Think of it like a high tide raising all boats. Here you are, Patricia, a little boat floating on the sea of human consciousness. While you can steer your boat to and fro, bring it to shore, or set out for deeper waters, you are still impacted by the water's level. You rise and fall depending on the tide. While you might be feeling relatively sure about who you are, if the waters of uncertainty and anxiety are rising in the collective whole of humanity, then (especially if you are tuned into the greater whole) you will start to feel uncertain and anxious yourself. You will likely at first not know why you are starting to feel unsettled; but if you start to take into consideration your interconnectedness, you might more easily recognize that your experience is arising from something bigger shifting around you.

Even more so, the tide of overall human development seems to be rising. There appears to be an awakening human consciousness that plays into our day-to-day lives. As a whole we are evolving. Not taking this into account would be like sailing a boat and thinking the rising and falling was based on the boat itself, not the tides.

Hour after hour, I meet with people who are having awakening experiences. They report becoming more conscious of themselves and their connection with the world. They realize that they are impacted by the sea of humanity, and are not just a little boat unto themselves. I don't think it is any coincidence that so many people are experiencing similar symptoms when it comes to expanding consciousness. Individuals have been reporting feelings of disorientation, an increased intensity in their emotions and dreams, and overall sudden changes happening in their internal and external world. Unusual aches and pains, increased sensitivity, a loss of identity, and sudden shifts in relationships all seem to be symptoms of a vast shift in the collective awareness.

It is not difficult for us to look at the outer world in general and see old paradigms falling away and new ones emerging. Changes to the political and cultural landscape, and the crumbling of established institutions in favor of more modern practices, are indicators of rapid movement happening globally. If we look at how quickly technological advances have been occurring, we might get a glimpse into our rapid expansion. Our ability to cram more information into smaller spaces has been doubly increasing each year since the 1960s. We have made more advances in technology in the last 150 years than we have throughout the previous course of recorded human history.

I think that this accelerating change in the rate of technological advancement is a reflection of the exponential growth happening in our overall human consciousness. We are becoming more and more awakened. Not taking this rapid change into account limits our understanding of what we are experiencing psychologically, both pleasant and unpleasant.

Patricia, it is like when your preteen daughter recently complained of growing pains. She described achy legs and knees that hurt. If you just took her knees into account, you would miss the fact that her entire body is growing and changing. Were you to bring her to an arthroscopic surgeon to treat knee pain, you would be missing the global growth of the body. Just like your daughter's achy legs were symptoms of larger growing pains, I hope you can see that the distress, doubt, and anxiety you feel in your little self might be due in part to the global shifts occurring in our larger collective consciousness.

Learning to see the bigger picture allows you to more masterfully weather these changes. When your own old ways of relating no longer work, perhaps you could see it as part of the falling away of old ways that people in general relate. The more we cling to those old structures, the more pain we will feel. Perhaps instead you could reinvent how you relate to yourself and others, and be a part of the rising tide of awakening consciousness.

Instead of clinging to old ways, can you find fluidity to roll with the changes of this modern world? Can you find a sort of divine surrender to what is occurring? I think of the Master Jedi Obi Wan Kenobi in the movie *Star Wars*. He knew that great changes were afoot in his world, and he worked to roll with them. In the first *Star Wars* movie, he fought a duel with the evil Darth Vader. He said to his nemesis, "If you strike me down, I shall become more powerful than you can possibly imagine." Obi Wan withdrew his light saber and was struck down by Darth Vader, leaving only his robe on the ground. Obi Wan merged with something bigger than him, "The Force," and was able to communicate to his apprentice Luke Skywalker from the beyond. He connected to the bigger picture and became more effective.

I use this as an example of not surrendering your life but instead seeing the bigger picture and learning how to be more fluid in how you relate to yourself and others. Where can you let go of old ways and step into the larger force that you are? Where can you bring old, outworn ways into the present time so that you can be on the front of the wave of human development? I know it is not an easy process, but if you see that it is not just you going through uncertain life changes, then you might be able to capture a bit of the adventure in the process.

Fondly yours,
David

Dear Eva,

The other day you asked me if I know where we are headed in our work together. We have been meeting for almost two years, and I think that you wanted to know if there is an overall goal. Each week you come in with interesting insights and various problems for us to address. Yet I understand that you want to know if there is an undergirding theme.

Sometimes our work together feels like playing whack-a-mole. One issue pops up over here and we address it. Then another problem pops up a week later over there, and we move over to handle that one. Maybe it feels like our meetings are more in reaction to occurrences in your life rather than a prescribed set of proactive, therapeutic interventions. I hear this from more clients than just you. People want a guiding narrative to their work in therapy, and to their lives in general. In your case, Eva, I would say that the overall theme boils down to separation. The root of your "whack-a-mole" issues can be traced back to a sense of feeling separated from the world.

Separation is a core issue for many of us. We feel different, or left out of groups. Our connection to nature seems removed, our participation in the world fleeting. We feel a profound sense of being "other than." It is a you-versus-me, or us-versus-them experience. So much of our social and political lives revolve around this sense of separation. Yet I'd like us to consider that this separation is an illusion.

Sigmund Freud, the father of psychoanalysis, essentially believed that our basic drives are sex and aggression. He said that what motivates us is primarily sexual intimacy or the desire to overpower others. I think that this is an outdated model of thinking about human desire. More modern thinking, stemming from the work of psychoanalyst Melanie Klein, is that our basic drives are for connection: we all deeply long to connect to something bigger than ourselves. Sex and aggression are ways of connecting, but there are many other ways such as hiking, meditating, communing with others, or being of service. However we pursue it, we long for connection. It is this built-in drive to connect which might be in response to a pervasive sense of separation plaguing the human mind. Whether to nature, other people, a cause, or something deeper within us, we all long to connect to something bigger than ourselves to alleviate this felt sense of separation.

I invite you, Eva, to look at where this might apply to you. Do you long for connection? Can you find where you are more closed off and in a state of separation, and try to find ways to gently, easily connect to something bigger than yourself? You report that people at work don't get you, that you are left out when they go to lunch together. You also talk about your sister-in-law regularly disregarding your needs. Last week you mentioned being at a fundraiser and not relating to anyone there. The week before that you talked about not ever being able to get outside to take a walk because there is too much work to do. Each painful example you share can be traced back to this underlying feeling of disconnectedness. Yet I think that separation is an illusion because, if you just start to notice, you may find that there are so many ways to connect to something bigger in your life. They are immediately accessible if we just remain open.

How can you find a way to stay open to connecting to life? Can you find other people, small moments, little links to something bigger than you? Can you even reach to something beyond the physical? Whether it is a mountain, the ocean, or your higher intelligence, can you touch the metaphysical and spiritual elements of life in order to span the chasm of separation which you experience on a daily basis? Psychology does not always address the spiritual, but at times we need to look at this part of ourselves in order to alleviate pervasive disconnection. Can you perhaps glimpse that on a particular level you are like the finger on your hand, which is connected to the other fingers on that hand, which is also part of the arm, which connects to the torso and the rest of the body. Spiritually speaking, can you see that you are a part of the larger whole … that you are a drop in the ocean, but at the same time part of the ocean itself?

What I am encouraging you to do is to cultivate a mindset of connectedness, rather than one of separation. See from the part of your mind which can glimpse into being one with humanity. What I have found is that without this mindset of unity that you will continually be pulled back into a felt sense of separation. No matter how many times we try to fix the group dynamics at your job, or problem-solve your relationship with your sister-in-law, or make you more socially graceful, or able to get out of work and go for a walk, we will still find another whack-a-mole situation popping up in which you feel disconnected. The solution to pervasive separation does not lie in trying to do something different about it, but rather to elevate your awareness to one which sees that you are part of something much bigger than yourself.

I wonder what it would be like to not feel separate from the world, but to instead see that you are as much a part of the world as your finger is a part of your hand. What would your relationships look like if you knew that on some level you are connected? Perhaps your search for connection would end, and you would turn toward building a relationship with whatever your source may be. How would life change if you believed the words of the Sufi poet Rumi?

He said, "You are not a drop in the ocean. You are the entire ocean in a drop."

Fondly yours,
David

Dear Kerry: Create a Sacred Space

Dear Kerry,

I keep thinking about your cliff-jumping story. This past summer on vacation in the American west, you went cliff jumping. The cliff wasn't too high and ended in a nice pool of water. You reported the cliff being high enough that it created a sense of anticipation and fear, but not too high that it was treacherous. Though you saw others jumping safely ahead of you, still you stood on the cliff's edge, hesitating, needing to muster the nerve to throw yourself into the waters below. It sounded terrifying.

I love how you connected this story to the dilemma you have been facing in your fear of public speaking. While everything within your evolutionary hardwiring tells you to back away from the cliff, you know that if you want to jump, you have to overcome the fear and throw yourself off. Just like public speaking goes against your instinctive tendency to hide, you are forced, because of work, to throw yourself in front of the crowd and open yourself up. Again, terrifying.

The longer you stood on the cliff's edge, the less likely you were to jump, as the hardwired fears kicked in and gained momentum to prevent you from taking the plunge. Similarly, the more you think about giving a talk, the more anxious you become. Yet to succeed at both of these scary endeavors, you have to take risks. You have to throw yourself in there against all primal conditioning. This sort of throwing ourselves into life is both thrilling and terrifying.

If you are going to take on a bold way of living, Kerry, then might I suggest you consider learning how to create sacred space? This might help with terrifying endeavors such as cliff jumping or public speaking, but also for day-to-day hallowed activities. A sacred space is any space or area that is designated for holy purposes. How we define holy can vary. Yet we know that the designation is for a specific purpose, rather than a more mundane, social, or leisurely pursuit. Sacred spaces are called upon for religious ceremony, meditation practices, or transformation rituals such as weddings and funerals. Their intentionality allows us to access extra support, safety, and skill when we venture onto the cliff edges of life.

When you delineate a sacred space, you are intentionally asking to alter your mindset. You are going from normal waking consciousness to a more profound place of purpose, wisdom, and love. For instance, when you are about to give a presentation for work, unless it is a greatly casual meeting, you shift into presentation mode. Likely you would not just waltz in there and wing it. Whether it is for an hour, or five minutes, or even five seconds before the presentation, you mark a shift from Everyday Kerry to Presenting Kerry in order to get into the right frame of mind.

Some people ring a bell, light a candle, or say a mantra when they enter their sacred space. The key is to intentionally delineate the mundane from the sacred. You might imagine drawing a line or a circle around the space and creating a boundary. When the circle is drawn, everything within it is sacred. All that takes place inside this circle can be done in a hallowed manner, while everything on the outside of the circle is secular. This holy circle can be imbued with the qualities you need for your endeavor. If it is a business presentation, then the interior of the circle can contain the qualities of learning, connection, understanding, and engagement. You might even call in the qualities of skillful oration, instruction, and clarity. Whichever attributes you summon, the key is to intentionally, through the creativity of your visualization, mark an appropriate mindset.

When we meet for a therapy session, I mark the space as sacred. I call upon sacred space before our sessions and ask that the time be imbued with compassion, connection, inspiration, and love. I call on skillful means for myself so that I am as understanding, in tune, grounded, clear, and insightful as I can be. I try not to just stroll into session in an ordinary mindset and hope for the best. Since I care deeply about our work, I aim to create a sacred space each time we meet. My hope is that you feel it the moment you walk into the room.

I encourage you, Kerry, to be masterful in this way. You can use sacred space not just at work, but at home and in your personal life. You can imagine that your home is delineated from the rest of the world as a peaceful abode. Imagine that circle around your house and summon the qualities that you would like in your home life. Some people will even draw on earthly or otherworldly forces to support their sacred space. Perhaps you could imagine the powers of the elements—earth, air, fire, and water—infusing your home. You might call in the support of the plant kingdom or animal kingdom to bring life to your house. Maybe there are higher powers, religious icons, or inspirational figures whose energy you would like to summon as well. However you charge your sacred space, the point is to make it your own, and create it in a way that is in the highest good for everyone involved.

Your sacred space does not need to just stay at home. You can create sacred spaces when you are traveling or in other locations. It can be a moveable feast that allows you to carry a felt sense of connectedness with you. It can be one that supports you and allows space for others as well. Again the key here is to intentionally delineate when you are moving from mundane to sacred. Your intentionality drives it.

You are certainly not required to call upon a sacred space in your daily life. Sometimes it is not needed. Yet other times it can help. Regardless of when you use it, an important element is to properly close the sacred space once your work is finished. You want to be sure to bring the space back to the mundane, and return yourself to ordinary waking consciousness. This allows the work to be ended, and for you to return to your life as usual. You could do this after a work presentation is finished. This is what I do when our session is over. I mentally note that the sacredness of the work is over and I move back to regular everyday life. This seals the work in place for the next time we meet and reopen the space. When your work is through, then move on to the next activity.

I think that this tool of creating a sacred space can make a difference for you, Kerry, as you develop self-mastery. It could be a big part of creating intentionality and taking personal responsibility for your life. The next time we meet, we can create the space together so that our work ever deepens.

Fondly yours,
David

PART XII
Transcending This Life

EXISTENTIAL REALITIES are always present in therapy. While they are not necessarily spoken aloud, the foundation of many people's distress is the awareness that at some point, hopefully way down the line, their lives are going to end. The fragility of life comes starkly into awareness when there is a great loss or tragedy that impacts us. People become shaken to their foundation when such realities come barging into their awareness.

Therapy does not really have any definitive answers to questions about death and dying. We can help comfort and soothe, we can be there together in the mystery, but therapists usually don't have any clear answers about how to handle death. We are on the same journey ourselves, trying to make sense of what would give our lives meaning. We grapple with the same questions, and aim to at least bring comfort and understanding when our clients face life's uncertainties.

Therapy does however offer some ways of thinking about living in the face of dying. We offer new perspectives that might help people take on their lives in more robust and satisfying ways. We can help people take a certain mindset that cultivates an expansive view of death. Helping people develop a connection to a practice of fully living might allow them to face death more bravely.

The little losses and deaths in life prepare us. Saying goodbye when relationships end, or when life causes separations, is really a challenge for many of us. It is not easy to say goodbye and know how to truly release those who we hold dear. Finding healthy ways to end attachments allows us to be open to new connections, yet much of our humanness keeps us bonded to past connections. Therapy aims to help us transcend some of the unhealthy ways we cling to others and to life itself.

These last few letters that follow are to clients who have been addressing some sort of transcendence in their lives. Either they are working to let go of a relationship, unplug from the demands of their day to day, or embrace a more truly transcendent spiritual practice. Each of them is grappling with some aspect of existential realities that impinge upon their lives. My hope is to help them move through these experiences with wisdom and grace.

Dear Stephanie,

I have to admit that I was frightened, and even overprotective, when you told me last month that you were going to Peru for an ayahuasca ceremony. You came nearly skipping into the office, letting me know that you had purchased your tickets and that you and a friend were going. You also wanted to know what I thought.

I don't really know that much about ayahuasca, but from what I have gathered it involves meeting with shamans and drinking the broth of the ayahuasca plant. This supposedly makes you vomit and have diarrhea for hours before you enter an altered state of consciousness. It is purported to open you up to insights about yourself that you might never find otherwise. People describe it as either intensely beautiful, very scary, or that nothing much happens.

It is exciting for me to work with people like you who are into this sort of adventure. Earlier this year you went on a ten-day vipassana retreat and came back having let go of many compulsive behaviors, such as your addiction to your phone, your severe lack of sleep, and an unhealthy relationship with one of your closest friends. I didn't know if the changes were going to stick, but to your credit they have. I was impressed. I enjoy witnessing how you let experiences like the retreat change you. Before the vipassana retreat you were on a women's empowerment weekend. Through psychodrama techniques you reclaimed your inner child, and have committed to weekly follow-up meetings with the women from the weekend. Last month you did a rebirthing experience in which, through deep breathing techniques, you were regressed to your birth and relived the trauma of coming through the birth canal. You described a blissful state of pre-birth memory, of being in the womb.

That is far out, but I like it. I believe that there is only so much that talk therapy can do. We need experiences that reach further into us, beyond language, and that help transform what no longer serves us. We live in a day and age in which there are so many opportunities available to the masses. Such esoteric experiences used to be reserved for mystics and royalty. Now all of us can consult healers, read books, watch videos, and have access to spiritual information.

All of this being said, last month you wanted to know what I thought of you going to Peru to do ayahuasca. You had already bought your tickets and I didn't want to burst your bubble. I tried to take as neutral a stance as possible, yet a voice inside of me said, "Enough already! Ayahuasca in Peru?! This has gone too far!"

What was this about? Why was I having such a strong reaction? You have continually proven a strength that can handle all sorts of experiences. Why was this latest one causing me to react so strongly? I think it is because it feels like you are searching for something that you can't find. You keep trying things further and further outside the box, yet you are still left restlessly seeking.

As far as I know, you are not Peruvian. You have not been raised in the Peruvian shamanic tradition. Unless you really surprise me, it does not seem that you will be inducted into the lineage of Peruvian shamanism. This ayahuasca ceremony seems like a novelty for you. It feels like another far-flung search for something that is right there within you. Rather than hallucinating on ayahuasca, how about firmly embedding yourself in an established spiritual practice and sticking with it?

You can see that I am not neutral about this. It is a bigger topic for me. I see too much spiritual materialism these days. It is fashionable to try spiritual work, to dabble in it. Yet what this world needs is the ordinary, everyday spiritual practitioner who embodies a commitment to their growth and the growth of others. I am encouraged by your interest in spiritual pursuits, but I wonder what it would be like for you to do less heavy-duty, mind-bending, consciousness- expanding activities, and just stick with an everyday practice of prayer and meditation. I have been told that prayer and meditation are the main vehicles for daily spiritual practice. Just like washing dishes, you do what needs to be done each day. There are not as many fireworks, just continual practice.

Being spiritual may look different for each person. I am not here to tell you how it is supposed to look for you, but I do know that a core aspect of spiritual practice is connecting with something beyond this life. We might consider meditation as a chance to transcend your day to day, and identify with something bigger than your mind and body. If you find a way to connect every day, then I think you will ease into an ever-present state of ease. You may not feel as much restless need to search far and wide for transcendent experiences because they will be available to you at home every day.

What matters more to me is not how many experiences you have that open up new insights, but how you *practice* being a spiritual person. Though you might not come skipping into session telling me about your 20 minutes of meditation that morning in which not that much happened, I know that I will feel the results of that daily work within you. I know that you will, too. Now it's time to wash the dishes.

Fondly yours,
David

Dear Alex: How to Really Unplug

Dear Alex,

It sounds to me like you need a vacation from your vacation. You just came back from a week away, and you seem exhausted. Holidays are meant to recharge us. They are a chance to unplug from the day-to-day grind, but your recent trip has left you even more frenzied. Coming back to an inbox full of emails and a pile of demands would make any of us want to get back on a plane and hide away for a few months.

You have created a full life for yourself, Alex, running a community center and being there for a team of employees on a regular basis. Your nonprofit has been making a difference in the world, and you have been carrying a majority of it on your weary shoulders. I know that your work is your passion, but your week away did nothing to alleviate the burnout and compassion-fatigue that you have been experiencing.

Yours is the malaise of the modern activist. You plug into so many important constructs that need your focus and attention, but you have a difficult time unplugging and replenishing. You told me how difficult it was to leave for vacation, and how anxious you were to be sure to meticulously tidy up everything before you boarded the plane. You reported feeling as if nothing at work would continue unless you were there to support its very existence.

As you know, this is unsustainable. Most people think that time on a beach or having a few cocktails will enable them to recharge. They hope that time in nature will do the trick, or exploring a new city might shake things up. Yet unless they know how to effectively separate out from their busy life, they will forever be consumed by it. Alex, you need to learn how to really unplug and replenish so that you can be more effective when you plug back in. I offer you at least one way that you can truly step out of all that you have going on in order to find some peace and quiet.

Look at where your attention is right now. Imagine for a moment that you have multiple points of attention that exist across space and time. Rather than just one point of awareness focused on a particular task, consider that there are aspects of your multifaceted mind that are attending to a myriad of people, plans, and projects. You are quite powerful in this way. Your attention is in hundreds, if not thousands, of places at once. This is all a part of living a rich life. Yet at times you would benefit from pulling your attention and awareness out of those places and honing it back on you.

When you were first preparing to open your community center, and the remodeling of the building interior was taking place, you were pouring all of your attention into the project. I know you had many sleepless nights worrying about how the construction was progressing. You attended to every detail of the process and communicated constantly with the project managers. You had so much attention on the project for weeks on end. The progress became stuck for days at a time, and you would call the foreman every day, yelling. The more you pushed the process, the more stuck it became. It was only when you diverted your attention to other projects that the construction moved along. Precisely when you unplugged, the process progressed.

How can we explain this? Why is it that what we are waiting for does not occur while we are concentrating on it? Why does a watched pot never boil? Perhaps because, somewhat magically, our attention keeps it from happening. When you were away on vacation, Alex, your body was away, but your mind was still very much here watching the pot boil. Being physically away but having your attention on work left you more here than you were there. In many ways you were neither here nor there! You were split.

To bring yourself into alignment, I suggest becoming aware that your life is where your attention is. If you are constantly attending to work, then your life becomes all about work. Calling your awareness and attention back to you—back to your body—brings your life back home. Rather than attending to a million things at once, try resting your attention on you, on your body, on your breath, for just a moment.

This is a process of centering that can help you in so many ways. It allows you a break from everything outside of you, while giving you a chance to approach your endeavors with more balance. It enables you to transcend the demands of your daily life and connect to your deeper self.

When an individual goes on a vision quest, they take on this process. They unplug from their daily life to connect to their deeper rhythms. In a way, they let their day-to-day lives die so that they can birth new ideas. This type of disengagement and replenishing is available to you even if you do not journey out into the bush for days. You can transcend this earthly life by practicing regular disengagement, discharging, and replenishing.

To do this, find some quiet time to pull your attention away from everything external. You could even imagine unplugging all the metaphorical cords you have plugged into various projects and people. Bring your attention onto yourself. Notice what you are feeling in your body. If there is any tension, stress, or places where you feel stuck, allow them to be released and discharged. You could imagine sitting on a tree stump and allowing all of your tension to drain down the roots of this tree into the earth. You can also imagine a thousand hands inside of you, holding onto everything so tightly. Allow all of those hands to release and let go at once, releasing down into the earth all the tension.

This is energetic discharging. It is becoming centered and grounded in a way that allows you more force to create your life. While you are letting everything leave your body, you allow a momentary vacation to accomplish much more than did your week away on the beach. You create new space within you for life to fill in. Instead of being consumed with constant demands and distractions, you allow room for becoming replenished.

If you can imagine a replenishing light shining down into you, filling you with your life force, then you will have taken steps to recharge your batteries. Much more so than lying in the sun on the beach, basking in the imagined light of your own life force brings you back into alignment. I try to do this practice each day. Being centered, clear of all the demands in life, and replenished with my own connection to life, allows me to be more fully present when I meet with you. It also allows me to unplug once our meeting ends. Without this process, I would not be able to sustain regular daily meetings.

Alex, I know you are up to so much in this world. You go charging into conscious projects with such gusto. Try as you might to take breaks and rejuvenate yourself, you continue to feel depleted. You fill up, then get drained, only to try to fill up once again. Instead of this back and forth process, try taking a bit of time on a regular basis to really unplug and replenish. Doing so, you transcend this life and tap into an unending reservoir of energy that can truly fuel you and all your precious endeavors.

Fondly yours,
David

Dear Allen: Bless and Release

Dear Allen,

Breakups are the worst. They bring so many people to therapy because of the great pain they cause. The loss of a significant relationship is often tremendously difficult to manage on one's own. I am glad that you reached out for help right after this breakup. You and your boyfriend had been together for eight formative years. You developed a sense of adult identity with one another. You describe it as a foundation bond that feels eternal. Losing such a core relationship can feel like the earth moving underneath your feet. Your world shakes as the bond between you breaks.

I don't see too many breakups that go really well. Seldom do two people mutually and peacefully decide to part ways. When they do it is usually because the relationship had really been over for quite some time. Yet your relationship, Allen, was going along well from all accounts until four months ago when your partner told you he had feelings for someone else. It caught you off guard, and even though he was willing to work on it with you for a while, the eventual loss sent you into some dark and painful places.

Breakups usually trigger past losses. They shake our usual sense of feeling securely connected with others. Where you previously felt you had a stable bond, you now unexpectedly are detached and alone. This can mimic small or large losses and abandonments from childhood. Slight neglect or rejection can make us doubt ourselves and our place in the world. When a breakup occurs in our adult life, it can elicit childhood wounds that bring with them a deep sense of powerlessness, anxiety, panic, or depression.

Attachment is a powerful thing. When an attachment bond is severed, it can break loose all sorts of intensity from our hearts. It can feel like we are coming unglued. All the self-care in the world may not be enough. Even if you spend time with good people in your life, look into what went wrong, find healing, and get back out there to meet new people, it can still be very difficult to truly move on from a relationship that has ended.

I have found that to really recover from a breakup, most people have to eventually get to a place where they can wish their ex well and fully release them. I call this the stance of blessing and releasing. By practicing a mindset of bless and release, you take steps to heal and recover from the relationship. No matter how badly your ex hurt or betrayed you, blessing them and releasing them is the surest path I have found for people to move forward into the next phase of their lives.

To bless someone means to truly wish them well. Could you imagine your ex living a satisfying and happy life? Could you find it within you to wish for him all good things? Would it be okay if you can imagine him being happy in a new, healthy relationship? This is often most difficult for people who feel betrayed by their partner, or who have some sense of unfinished business. They want the score to be settled, and to somehow win the breakup. They want their partner to be unhappy and for them to realize what a mistake they made. Such feelings are normal, but they do not ultimately serve you very well. The best revenge is living well, so perhaps you could find a way to wish your ex well, and move on to create a good life for yourself.

This is easier said than done, so I prescribe for you a daily practice of blessing your ex so that he lives a good life. Ultimately, beyond all the drama and lovers' quarrels, don't you want your ex to be well? Person to person, do you not, deep down, want all the best for this other human being with whom you shared so much? I ask you to try to find that deeper place within you that can bless him.

What makes this difficult is that you are still holding onto him. You cling to the past and to what you used to have. You want to see some sort of justice or resolution to the unfinished business of the relationship. Most relationships do not end cleanly. Breakups are messy, and unless you want to keep wading in the mess, I encourage you to practice releasing your ex. By blessing and releasing him, you step into a much more powerful place. You become the one bestowing blessings rather than clinging in pain. You are the one choosing to release, rather than blaming. If you practice blessing and releasing, I think you will find that you will feel stronger and your heart will start healing. Moreover, you can claim a powerful attitude toward life overall.

Blessing and releasing can be used not just in breakups, but in any sort of ending in life. When you leave someone, or a situation, what do you want to give them before you go? Can you lend an insight, a word of lovingkindness, well wishing, or encouragement? That is the blessing. It is an offering that you set forth to others involved. This attitude of giving differs from a more common attitude of looking at what you can take from the situation. Instead of asking, "What did I get out of it?" look instead at what did you bestow to others. This mindset will benefit everyone involved, and will also feel good for you.

Once your interaction is complete, and you have blessed those involved, then release. In your mind, work to completely end the encounter. Letting go and ending the interaction allows it to be over, and enables you to stay present. Too many of us drag around past interactions, obsessively thinking about them. With our minds in the past, the interactions do not end.

There is a difference between things ending and them stopping. Your relationship stopped months ago, but it has not ended in your mind. In a way it still lives on inside you. Alternatively, a relationship can end well before it stops. Many people drag their relationships out for years, not putting it to rest, even though for all intents and purposes it has long since ended. Allen, your relationship stopped a little way back. Though it might be sad, your work now is to release it so that it can fully end.

There are many ways to end a relationship. Many cultures have rituals to say goodbye. Funerals are an example of how we formally say goodbye to loved ones once they pass. A lot of cultures have rituals that include three primary aspects: saying thank you, saying "I'm sorry," and saying goodbye. To close a relationship, we can find ways to express our gratitude for what we have shared, and to thank the others for how we have benefited from the encounter. In some way, we also try to say "I'm sorry." We ask for forgiveness for how we have fallen short or let others down in our time with them. We acknowledge and take accountability for how we may have gotten it wrong. This allows for others to get complete as well. Lastly, we say goodbye. We find a way to end the time together. Rather than, "so long," or "see you around," we say a full goodbye to formally stop the encounter. These three practices—thank you, I'm sorry, and goodbye—are foundational for how we might consciously find an ending. We don't necessarily need to say these things to the other person out loud. Having an inner dialogue with them suffices.

An example of an internal ritual of reconciliation and forgiveness that I like is the ancient Hawaiian practice of Ho'oponopono. While it has its roots in healing practices throughout the South Pacific, an updated version of Ho'oponopono includes four steps. They are repentance, forgiveness, gratitude, and love. When one practices Ho'oponopono, they say to the other person, "I'm sorry, please forgive me, thank you, and I love you." Again this can be said in person, or even just in your own mind. By truly feeling sorry for the hurts you have caused, by humbly asking for forgiveness, by thanking the other person for who they are, and last, by expressing your love for them, you shift to a powerful, humble, and gracious stance in your release of the relationship. It is a beautiful way to say goodbye.

Allen, however you choose to work through this breakup, I am here to support you. Grieving a loss is not easy, and I encourage you to be kind to your aching heart and gentle with the pain you are enduring. I usually see it taking about two months after the breakup for the intense hurting to subside. Take time for yourself, but let us also see if we can find a way for you to practice blessing and releasing your former love. By doing so, I am positive that you will find relief. Plus you will be more prepared to encounter the future goodbyes in life that are sure to come.

Fondly yours,
David

Dear Toni: Be Ahead of All Parting

Dear Toni,

It is supposed to be useful to think about death each day. Without it consuming us, regular thoughts of death are believed to help us with feeling more fully alive. Wrestling with the mystery of living and dying builds a certain awareness that lifts life out of the mundane. While I would not propose you become absorbed in thinking about dying, you might find that against a backdrop of existential awareness, your life stands out more fully.

Toni, you are at a stage in life where I hear you contemplating your purpose. You are looking back on your 50 years of life and wondering what it has meant. More than a midlife crisis, I hear you struggling with finding meaning in the face of meaninglessness. You have had enough success in family and business, and made compromises along the way, but have found enough of a sense of what matters to you. With your children growing up, you have reported thinking more about your own mortality lately. The week you spent waking up in the middle of the night, afraid of dying, might have marked a shift into a new awareness of what matters to you.

Death puts our daily agitation and stress into perspective. Rather than becoming lost in the minutia of our humdrum lives, an awareness of the impermanence of things has made you contemplate the substance of your existence. It has opened up a new perspective. Early twentieth-century Austrian poet and novelist Rainer Maria Rilke wrote of this perspective in his *Sonnets to Orpheus* from 1922.

> *Be ahead of all parting as though it already were behind you, like the winter that has just gone by. For among these winters there is one so endlessly winter that only by wintering through it all will your heart survive. Be forever dead in Eurydice—more gladly arise into the seamless life proclaimed in your song. Here, in the realm of decline, among momentary days, be the crystal cup that shattered even as it rang.*[9]

Without being overly morbid, this "being ahead of all parting" can become an expanded outlook on life. Rilke prompts us to be prepared and awake, rather than blissfully entranced by the illusions of life. Being forever dead in Eurydice suggests a more transcendent approach to your own being. It lifts you from focusing on only what is right in front of you, and pulls you into a contemplation of what is really important.

In a way, Toni, you have been contemplating your legacy. You have been wondering how you will be remembered and what you will leave behind. Will you be remembered as someone who got all the chores done, and someone who always made reliable decisions? Or are you prepared to go for something bigger? You have been wondering how you will leave your mark; if you were to die soon, you wonder if you would leave any sort of lasting memory.

This is weighty stuff, but worth taking on. Our to-do lists, and endless demands on our attention from media, can distract us from significant existential and philosophical musings. Your adult years have been filled with building your family and career, and driving yourself to be your best. You have erected your life from the ground up. Yet now it might be time, in the realm of decline, to look at your momentary days, to live your life fully, and as Rilke suggests, to find your ringing amidst the shattering.

Shakespeare's *Romeo and Juliet* gives us a taste of this perspective. We learn in the prologue that this is a tale of two "star-cross'd lovers" who "take their life." We know before the story commences that it will end in death, yet we are transfixed by watching these two shining stars flame out. Their lives, against the awareness of impending demise, burn brightly. Just like a falling star burning up in the Earth's atmosphere, we are inspired by how life can shine as it starts to end.

The final act is usually the most compelling. Toni, you have plenty of time to cement your legacy. There are chapters yet unwritten. If you keep your head down and just focus on your daily tasks and to-do lists, you might wake up in twenty more years and still wonder what your purpose is. However, if you keep utilizing the small, quiet moments to contemplate living and dying, you might find lasting meaning.

Think of how you feel when you are sitting around a campfire and watching the last burning embers. You know that the fire is on the verge of becoming extinguished, but you can't help but being entranced by the glowing cinders. When the flames roar, we chatter and cavort around the fire pit. Yet in those closing moments, it is usually silent for a reason. The ending speaks something deep to us, like a sunset or the last days of autumn.

We are moved by the dying light, for in it is the concentration of life force. Living beings give their last burst of energy as they meet their end. You, Toni, are nowhere near the end, but your recent obsessive thoughts about death may be calling you to fight the shadows and increase your light. While it might seem paradoxical, your thinking about dying is a call to start living.

Fondly yours,
David

ENDNOTES

[1]Rogers, CR. *The necessary and sufficient conditions for therapeutic personality change*. Journal of Consulting Psychology 1957;21:97-103.

[2] Osho, (2008). Being in Love: How to Love with Awareness and Relate Without Fear. New York: Harmony Books, 2008.

[3]Lao Tzu. (1972). Tao Te Ching. New York: Vintage Books

[4]V Kumari et al. (2017). *Brain connectivity changes occurring following cognitive behavioural therapy for psychosis predict long-term recovery*. Translational Psychiatry.

[5]Moyne, J & Barks, C (1984). *Open Secret: Versions of Rumi*. Threshold Books.

[6]Niebuhr, R., & Brown, R. M. A. (1986). *The Essential Reinhold Niebuhr: Selected Essays and Addresses*. New Haven: Yale University Press.

[7]Goldenberg, I. & Goldenberg, H. (1991). *Family therapy: An overview* (3rd ed.). Belmont, CA: Brooks/Cole.

[8]Rilke, R. (1996). *Uncollected Poems*: Bilingual Edition. New York: North Point Press.

[9]Rilke, R. M., Cohn, S., & Rilke, R. M. (2000). *Sonnets to Orpheus, with Letters to a Young Poet*. Manchester, England: Carcanet.

ACKNOWLEDGEMENTS

I gratefully acknowledge the support and assistance that I have received from countless individuals over the years. Your love and encouragement has lead to the creation of this book. Thank you to Nancy Cleary at Wyatt-MacKenzie Publishing for having the vision to see the value in this book, and for helping bring these letters into the world. I appreciate Nancy's willingness to provide writers and entrepreneurs the ability to have a joy-filled, viable, and empowered publishing experience. Thank you to Alexandra Solomon for supporting and encouraging me, and for lending your warmth and wisdom to the foreword for this book.

I know that I would not be doing what I do without the massive help of the supervisors and mentors who have shepherded me along over the years. Chief among them are Linda Rubinowitz and Marina Eovaldi. Along with the team at The Family Institute at Northwestern University, Linda and Marina's commitment to the field of Marriage and Family Therapy, and to training clinicians, has made a lasting impact on me and my work.

I am grateful for the training and development that I have received over the years from Shelley Amdur. She has poured her love and support into my growth as a person and a healer. She has a huge hand in shaping the idea for this book. Thank you also to Ken and Natalia Jones for helping open my eyes, and to Lou Weiss for first showing me what a loving therapist looks like.

I am also forever indebted to my parents, brother Jordan, family, friends and loved ones who have stuck by me while I have grown and changed over the years. Being a therapist and healer is not an easy road, and I have been sustained by the friendship and love I have received from them. A special thank you to Jerome Greenwald and Heather Feinberg for your ongoing friendship, ideas, warmth and support…and to Angelica for finally coming into my life when I needed you most.

Last but not least, I want to thank all of the clients that I have worked with over the years. Your courage and willingness to take on the hard work of therapy has truly inspired me. I am honored that you have opened yourselves up to me in session and been willing to share the depth of your struggles. This book is for you.

David Klow
Chicago, Illinois

ABOUT THE AUTHOR

David Klow is the founder and owner of Skylight Counseling Center in Chicago. He is a Licensed Marriage and Family Therapist. He is also extensively trained as an intuitive healer and spiritual guide in the lineage of the School of Spiritual Cycles as well as in the tradition of the Berkeley Psychic Institute. David works creatively and collaboratively, drawing on ancient wisdom and modern practices to bring lasting transformation to people's lives and the world.

David created Skylight Counseling Center in 2011, which is dedicated to the growth and development of individuals, couples and families. Combining traditional psychotherapy and spiritual healing, Skylight helps hundreds of people annually to find deeper passion and meaning in their lives. Through Skylight, David has been bringing forth new modalities of treatment which are helping to take psychotherapy into its next era.

David is a Clinical Lecturer through the Department of Psychology for Northwestern University's Master of Science in Marital and Family Therapy Program at The Family Institute. David is also a Clinical Member of and Approved Supervisor through The American Association for Marriage and Family Therapy. He received his Master of Science in Marital and Family Therapy from The Family Institute at Northwestern University along with extensive advanced training in The Family Institute Post-Graduate Clinical Fellowship. Today David runs Skylight, manages his expanding clinical staff, offers numerous professional trainings and workshops, and sees clients on a regular basis.

www.skylightcounselingcenter.com

INDEX

G

H

I

J

K

L

M

N

O

P

CPSIA information can be obtained
at www.ICGtesting.com
Printed in the USA
BVHW03s0332160218
508099BV00002B/129/P